THE WAR OF 1812

THE WAR OF
1812

A SHORT HISTORY

DONALD R. HICKEY

UNIVERSITY OF ILLINOIS PRESS

Urbana and Chicago

Illini Books edition, 1995

© 1995 by the Board of Trustees of the University of Illinois
Manufactured in the United States of America
P 5 4 3 2

This book is printed on acid-free paper.

Library of Congress Cataloging-in-Publication Data

Hickey, Donald R., 1944–
    The War of 1812 : a short history / Donald R. Hickey.
        p.   cm.
    Includes bibliographical references (p.   ) and index.
    ISBN 0-252-06430-5 (pbk. : alk. paper)
    1. United States—History—War of 1812. I. Title.
    E354.H535   1995
    973.5'2—dc20   94-17031
                                                   CIP

For
Bob McColley, who taught me history,
and
Mort Borden, who taught me how to write history

Contents

PREFACE

This book is a condensed version of my study *The War of 1812: A Forgotten Conflict*, which was published by the University of Illinois Press in 1989. That work enjoyed a fairly wide audience, mainly through the Book-of-the-Month Club and the History Book Club. My aim here is to present the essentials of that study in abbreviated form.

The original work was 118,000 words and included 115 pages of notes. I have dropped the notes and trimmed the text by almost two-thirds—to about 40,000 words. Most of the cuts were made in the domestic history, although I also compressed the diplomatic history and eliminated some details from the military and naval campaigns. I have modernized the capitalization, spelling, and punctuation of all contemporary quotations. I have also added a chronology. As in the original study, the maps have been put at the end of the text to facilitate use.

For helpful criticisms of an early draft of this work, I am indebted to Vance Burke, Connie Clark, and Bob McColley.

INTRODUCTION

The War of 1812 is probably our most obscure war. Although a great deal has been written about the conflict, the average American is only vaguely aware of why we fought or who the enemy was. Even those who know something about the contest are likely to remember only a few dramatic moments, such as the Battle of New Orleans, the burning of the nation's capital, or the writing of "The Star-Spangled Banner."

Why is this war so obscure? One reason is that no great president is associated with the conflict. Although his enemies called it "Mr. Madison's War," James Madison hardly measures up to such war leaders as Abraham Lincoln, Woodrow Wilson, or Franklin Roosevelt. In addition, the great generals in this war—Andrew Jackson and Winfield Scott—were unable to turn the tide because each was confined to a secondary theater of operations. No one like George Washington, Ulysses Grant, or Dwight Eisenhower emerged to put his stamp on the war and carry the nation to victory.

Another reason for the obscurity of this war is that (like many wars) its causes are complex and still subject to debate. Some scholars have argued for the primacy of maritime causes, claiming that the United States went to war to force the British to give up the Orders in Council and impressment. In contemporary parlance, the war was fought for "free trade and sailors' rights." Other writers have emphasized western aims—the desire to conquer Canada to secure additional farmland or to put an end to British influence over American Indians. Still others have focused on political causes, asserting that the Republicans embraced war as a means of forging party unity, maintaining power, and silencing the Federalists. Yet another group has stressed ideological factors—the desire to uphold the prestige of the Republic, preserve national honor, and ensure the continued vitality of republican institutions. The decision for war, in other words, has been attributed to a wide variety of motives.

If the causes of the war are unclear, so too are the consequences. The United States has won most of its wars, often emerging with significant concessions from the enemy, but the War of 1812 was different. Far from bringing the enemy to terms, the nation was lucky to escape without making extensive concessions itself. The Treaty of Ghent (which ended the conflict) said nothing about the issues that had caused the war and contained nothing to suggest that the United States had achieved its aims. Instead, it merely provided for returning to the *status quo ante bellum*—the state of affairs existing before the war.

The prosecution of the war was marred by considerable bungling and mismanagement. This was partly due to the nature of the Republic. The nation was too young and immature—and its government too feeble and inexperienced—to prosecute a major war efficiently. Politics also played a part. Federalists vigorously opposed the conflict, and so did some Republicans. Even those who supported the war feuded among themselves and never displayed the sort of patriotic enthusiasm that has been so evident in most other wars the United States has fought. The advocates of war appeared to support the conflict with their heads more than with their hearts, and with their hearts more than with their purses. As a result, efforts to recruit men and raise money lagged consistently behind need.

Despite the bungling and half-hearted support that characterized this conflict, the War of 1812 was not without its stirring moments and splendid victories. The crushing defeat of the British at New Orleans, the rousing defense of Baltimore, and the naval triumphs on the northern lakes and the high seas all showed that with proper leadership and training American fighting men could hold their own against the well-drilled and battle-hardened regulars of Great Britain.

The war also produced its share of heroes—people whose reputations were enhanced by military or government service. The war helped catapult four men into the presidency—Andrew Jackson, John Quincy Adams, James Monroe, and William Henry Harrison—and three men into the vice presidency—Daniel D. Tompkins, John C. Calhoun, and Richard M. Johnson. The war also gave a significant boost to the political or military careers of other men, most notably Henry Clay, Jacob

Brown, and Winfield Scott. Indeed, for many ambitious young men, the war offered an excellent launching pad for a career.

In some ways the War of 1812 looked to the past more than to the future. As the second and last war the United States fought against Great Britain, it echoed the ideology and issues of the American Revolution. It was the second and last time that the United States was the underdog in a war and the second and last time that the nation tried to conquer Canada. The war was unique in generating such vigorous political opposition and nearly unique in ending in a draw. Although most Americans pretended they had won the war—even calling it a "second war of independence"—they could point to few concrete gains to support this claim.

It is this lack of success that may best explain why the war is so little remembered. Americans have characteristically judged their wars on the basis of their success. The best-known wars—the Revolution, the Civil War, and World War II—were all spectacular successes. Although many people remembered the War of 1812 as a success, it was actually a failure, and perhaps this is why it attracts so little attention today.

The obscurity of this war, however, should not blind us to its significance, for it was an important turning point, a great watershed, in the history of the young Republic. It concluded almost a quarter of a century of troubled diplomacy and partisan politics and ushered in the Era of Good Feelings. It marked the end of the Federalist party but the vindication of Federalist policies, many of which were adopted by Republicans during or after the war. It also broke the power of American Indians and reinforced the powerful undercurrent of Anglophobia that had been present in American society since the Revolution. Above all, it promoted national self-confidence and encouraged the heady expansionism that lay at the heart of American foreign policy for the rest of the century. Although looking to the past, the war was fraught with consequences for the future, and for this reason it is worth studying today.

1

THE COMING OF THE WAR, 1801–12

On March 4, 1801, Thomas Jefferson walked from his boardinghouse in Washington City, as the nation's capital was then called, to the capitol building, where he was inaugurated as third president of the United States. The inauguration was short and spartan. The nation's new leaders favored a more democratic style than their Federalist predecessors. They also planned to adopt a new set of policies. It was these policies—initiated by Jefferson and carried on by his friend and successor, James Madison—that put the United States on a collision course with Great Britain and ultimately led to the War of 1812.

Republicans did not differ with Federalists over the broad objectives of American policy in this era. The French Revolution erupted in the summer of 1789 and led to a long series of Anglo-French wars that lasted from 1793 to 1815. During this era of sustained warfare, all Americans agreed that the United States should work to promote prosperity at home while protecting its rights and preserving its neutrality abroad. But what was the best way to achieve these ends? It was this question, more than any other, that divided Americans into two political camps.

Federalists subscribed to the old Roman doctrine, proclaimed and popularized by George Washington and Alexander Hamilton, that held that the best way to preserve peace was to prepare for war. Toward this end, they implemented a broad program of financial and military preparedness when they were in power from 1789 to 1801. Besides adopting Hamilton's financial program (which called for a broad-based tax system, a funded national debt, and a national bank), they expanded the army, built a navy, and initiated a system of coastal fortifications. Their aim was not only to deter war but also to put the nation in a position to defend itself in case of hostilities.

Besides promoting preparedness at home, the Federalists pursued a pro-British foreign policy. The cornerstone of this policy was the Jay Treaty of 1794, an Anglo-American agreement that regulated commerce and defined belligerent and neutral rights in time of war. The Republicans denounced this treaty—one newspaper called it the "death-warrant to our neutral rights"—but there is no denying that it achieved two important ends. It ensured peace with the one nation whose naval power could menace the United States, and it ushered in an era of Anglo-American accord that allowed American commerce—and hence the American economy—to flourish. American exports, which stood at $33 million in 1794, soared to $94 million in 1801, and the entire nation basked in the resulting prosperity.

The only liability of the Jay Treaty was that it was deeply resented by the French, who regarded it as a betrayal of the alliance that had bound them to the United States since the American Revolution. France responded to the treaty by severing diplomatic relations and unleashing its warships and privateers on American commerce. This led to the Quasi-War, an undeclared naval war that lasted from 1798 to 1801. The Federalist navy acquitted itself well in this war. Cruising mainly in the Caribbean, where most of the French depredations had occurred, the navy defeated several French warships, captured many French privateers, and recaptured a large number of American merchant vessels. As a result, France called off its war on American commerce and agreed to the restoration of peace.

In spite of the success of Federalist policies, the Federalists' approach to politics was too elitist for this era of rising democracy, and their foreign policy was too pro-British for a people whose experiences during the Revolutionary War had left them with an abiding hatred of England. In addition, some of the measures adopted during the Quasi-War—particularly the excise taxes and the alien and sedition laws—were unpopular with many Americans, and this contributed to the defeat of the Federalists in the election of 1800.

❖ ❖ ❖ ❖ ❖

When the Republicans took office in 1801, they began to reverse the policies they had inherited from the Federalists. Convinced that the excise taxes and the national bank discriminated against their constituents in the South and West, they got rid of these measures as soon as they could. They also trimmed the army and navy, preferring instead to rely on the militia and privateers as well as small and inexpensive gunboats. In addition, they used the officer corps of the army as a dumping ground for the party faithful.

The Republican policy of retrenchment was popular with most Americans, and at least initially it did little harm. England and France concluded the Peace of Amiens in late 1801 and remained at peace until 1803. When the European war resumed, however, both belligerents began to violate American rights and prey on its commerce. With their huge fleet, the British controlled the high seas, and Americans found their behavior particularly obnoxious. Soon a whole range of issues emerged that drove the two English-speaking nations apart.

To fill out their crews, British warships periodically stopped American merchant vessels on the high seas and impressed or drafted seamen into British service. Although impressment was supposed to be limited to British subjects, by accident or design an estimated 6,000 Americans were caught in the British dragnet between 1803 and 1812. British officials were willing to release impressed Americans, but only after satisfactory proof of their citizenship had been delivered through diplomatic channels, a process that could take years. In the meantime, American victims of impressment were forced to serve on British warships and were exposed to all the rigors of a harsh discipline and all the dangers of a war that was not their own.

Besides impressing seamen from American ships, the British infringed upon other American rights. They periodically interfered with America's lucrative trade with the West Indies and often violated American territorial waters, searching and seizing American vessels within the three-mile limit. In addition, they made sweeping use of naval blockades and insisted on a much broader definition of contraband than Americans were willing to concede.

The British offered to resolve some of these problems in the Monroe-Pinkney Treaty of 1806. This treaty was designed to be a successor to the Jay Treaty and in fact was even more favorable to the United States, but President Jefferson found it so unsatisfactory (mainly because it ignored impressment) that he refused to submit it to the Senate. The loss of the Monroe-Pinkney Treaty was an important turning point. By rejecting this treaty, the United States missed an opportunity to reforge the Anglo-American accord of the 1790s and to take the road that led to peace and prosperity instead of one that led to commercial restrictions and war.

After the loss of the Monroe-Pinkney Treaty, Anglo-American relations steadily deteriorated. In the summer of 1807 there was a full-blown war scare when the British warship *Leopard* fired on the American warship *Chesapeake,* killing and wounding a number of the crew. After the *Chesapeake* surrendered, a British press-gang forcibly removed several alleged British deserters. The British government never claimed the right to impress from neutral warships (which were considered an extension of a nation's territory), and it disavowed the attack and offered compensation. Nevertheless, the issue became entangled with others, and a settlement was delayed until 1811. In the meantime, the *Chesapeake* affair festered, contributing to the rising tide of anti-British feeling in the United States.

Shortly after the *Chesapeake* outrage, another problem surfaced that was to bedevil Anglo-American relations even more. This was the Orders in Council, a series of decrees issued by the British government that required neutral trade with the European continent to pass through England. The British defended the Orders in Council as a necessary response to Napoleon's Continental Decrees, which prohibited neutral trade with the British Isles. This did little to pacify Americans, who thought the European belligerents were using their war as a pretext for looting American commerce. American losses were considerable. Between 1807 and 1812 England, France, and their allies seized about nine hundred American ships.

In response to the growing infringements on American rights, the Republicans imposed a series of economic sanctions. Known collectively as the restrictive system, these measures grew out of the Republican belief that the nation's commerce was its greatest weapon. Aimed primarily at England and secondarily at France, the restrictive system was designed to force the European belligerents to show greater respect for American rights.

In 1806 Congress enacted a partial nonimportation act that prohibited certain British imports. The following year Congress added a general embargo that barred all exports. In 1809 Congress dropped these measures and substituted a nonintercourse act that prohibited all trade with Britain, France, and their colonies. This law was repealed in 1810, and the following year Congress imposed a nonimportation act that barred all British imports. These measures failed to win any concessions from the belligerents. Instead, they boomeranged on the United States, undermining its prosperity and depriving the federal government of much-needed revenue from trade. American exports, which had peaked at $108 million in 1807, plummeted to $22 million in 1808. The effect on the American economy was disastrous.

Two other developments contributed to the deterioration of Anglo-American relations in 1811. The first was the *Little Belt* incident, a kind of *Chesapeake* affair in reverse, in which the American warship *President* fired on the British warship *Little Belt,* killing or wounding several of the crew.

The other development was the outbreak of an Indian war on the northwestern frontier. The hostile Indian confederation was headed by two Shawnee leaders, Tecumseh and his brother Tenskwatawa (better known as the Prophet), who were determined to renounce the ways of whites and prevent further encroachments on their lands. Most Americans were convinced that British officials in Canada were behind the Indian conspiracy. "We have had but one opinion as the cause of the depredations of the Indians," said *Niles' Register;* "they are instigated and supported by the British in Canada."

In late 1811 William Henry Harrison defeated the Indians in the Battle of Tippecanoe in present-day Indiana. Indian depredations, however, continued to render the entire Northwest unsafe. "Most of the citizens in this country," Harrison reported in 1812, "have abandoned their farms and taken refuge in such temporary forts as they have been able to construct."

❖ ❖ ❖ ❖ ❖

By the time the Twelfth Congress—known to history as the War Congress—convened on November 4, 1811, there was growing talk of war with England. The British had made no concessions on the matters in dispute, and any settlement of the leading issues—the Orders in Council and impressment—seemed as remote as ever. Many Americans were also frustrated with the restrictive system, which seemed to do more damage to the United States than to either belligerent.

The Republicans had solid majorities in both houses of the new Congress, controlling 75 percent of the seats in the House and 82 percent in the Senate. Yet for years they had been without competent floor leadership and beset by factionalism. The regular Republicans, who customarily followed the administration's lead, could usually muster a majority, but sometimes dissident members of the party combined with Federalists to thwart administration measures. "Factions in our own party," complained one Republican, "have hitherto been the bane of the Democratic administration."

Fortunately for the administration, there was a new faction in the War Congress capable of providing the leadership and firmness that hitherto had been lacking. These were the War Hawks, a group of ardent patriots—men too young to remember the horrors of the last British war and thus willing to run the risks of another to vindicate the nation's rights. There were about a dozen War Hawks, most of whom came from the South or West.

The most able and articulate of the War Hawks was Henry Clay of Kentucky. Although not yet thirty-five and never before a member of the House, Clay was elected speaker and lost no time establishing his authority. He molded the speakership into a position of power and (as one contemporary put it) "reduced the chaos to order." By directing debate, interpreting the rules, packing key committees, and acting forcefully behind the scenes, Clay ensured that the War Hawks dominated the Twelfth Congress.

The president sent his annual message to the new Congress on November 5, 1811. Focusing on the Orders in Council, Madison accused England of making "war on our lawful commerce" and called on Congress to put the nation "into an armor and an attitude demanded by the crisis." Congress responded by adopting the most comprehensive program of war preparations since the Quasi-War. The army was expanded, and the recruitment of short-term volunteers and the use of the militia were authorized. Money was appropriated for the purchase of ordnance and the construction of coastal fortifications. Congress also voted to prepare all warships for service, though it refused to expand the fleet. In addition, Congress authorized a war loan and endorsed (but did not adopt) new taxes.

Although most of the war preparations were adopted by large majorities, the voting masked deep-seated differences among the various factions. The War Hawks supported these measures as a prelude to war; Republicans from commercial districts supported them because they had long advocated stronger defense measures. In addition, there were some Republicans—the "scarecrow" party—who supported war preparations in the hope of frightening the British into concessions. The Republicans were also divided over what kind of troops to raise. Some favored long-term regulars, others short-term volunteers, still others the militia. They also disagreed over the wisdom of naval expansion and new taxes. New taxes might be necessary, but they were sure to be unpopular.

The Federalists offered little resistance to the war measures and even voted for some of them. They were anxious to avoid the charge that they were under the influence of Great Britain, and they were determined to uphold their tradition of military and naval preparedness. Moreover, on the issue of naval expansion, they went much further than the Republicans. Unlike most Republicans, who wanted to fight a British war in Canada, the Federalists believed that the best place to defend the nation's maritime rights was on the high seas. "If you had a field to defend in Georgia," said Congressman Josiah Quincy, "it would be very strange to put up a fence in Massachusetts. And yet, how does this differ from invading Canada, for the purpose of defending our maritime rights?"

In spite of these differences, the Republican war program was impressive—at least on paper. The War Hawks hoped that the program would prepare the American people psychologically and militarily for war. President Madison hoped for the same result, and he used the powers of his office to stimulate the war spirit. On March 9, 1812, as the war program was nearing completion, he informed Congress of a British plot to incite disunion in Federalist New England. To support this claim, the president submitted documents acquired from a British spy named John Henry, who had visited New England in 1808 and 1809.

The semiofficial Washington *National Intelligencer* expressed hope that Henry's papers would "become a bond of union against a common foe," but their effect was just the opposite. Close examination of the documents revealed that Henry had implicated no one but had simply reported to British officials on political conditions in New England. Federalists were furious over this attempt to impugn their loyalty. Moreover, by tracing warrants from the Treasury Department, they soon discovered that the documents had been purchased for the princely sum of $50,000—rather than freely given, as Henry's cover letter had implied. This only added to the Federalists' outrage and to the embarrassment of Republicans.

In early April of 1812, just as the dust raised by the Henry affair was settling, Congress took another step toward war by enacting a ninety-day embargo and a ninety-day nonexportation law. Together, these measures prohibited American ships from clearing for foreign ports and barred the export of all goods and money by land or sea. The War Hawks promoted this legislation as a forerunner to war. If the USS *Hornet*, which was expected from Europe shortly, did not bring news of British concessions, the War Hawks were determined to plunge the nation into war.

The War Hawks insisted that the new laws were designed to protect American property by keeping all ships and cargo in port. Most Americans, however, refused to believe that war was near. News of the laws led to a flurry of activity as merchants in every port rushed to get their ships to sea. Freight rates jumped 20 percent, and many vessels were wholly loaded in two days. Republicans no less than Federalists took part in the frenzied activity. "In this *hurley burley* to palsy the arm of the government," *Niles' Register* conceded, "justice compels us to say that all parties united."

The rush to get ships to sea made a mockery of the whole war movement. "The great body of the people," said *Niles' Register*, "have acted as though an adjustment of differences with Great Britain, instead of an appeal to the sword, was at hand." Insurance rates—a good indication of public expectations—remained low in early 1812, even for ships sailing to England. "We hear from all quarters," wrote a War Hawk in late March, "that the people do not expect war."

Federalists were particularly skeptical of the war talk. In a highly publicized speech delivered in 1809, Josiah Quincy of Massachusetts had claimed that the Republican majority "could not be kicked into" war. Nothing in the years that followed had altered Quincy's opinion. Even after the War Congress had assembled, Quincy claimed that the talk of war was "ludicrous" and that even "the highest toned of the war party" conceded privately that hostilities were unlikely. Most Federalists shared this view.

The government was partly responsible for this skepticism. Talk of war in the past had never led to hostilities, and the signals emanating from the administration continued to be mixed. As late as March 31 Secretary of State James Monroe, sounding very much like a proponent of the scarecrow strategy, told a House committee that the war preparations were designed mainly to "*appeal to the feelings of the [British] government.*" The administration also kept the British minister, Augustus J. Foster, in the dark. By early May Foster was so confused by the signals he was receiving that he wrote to a British consul: "so absolutely are they here without chart or compass that I really am at a loss to give you news."

Republicans in Congress were also sending mixed signals. "The war fever," reported a House Federalist, "has its hot and cold fits." It was well known that some Republicans had voted for the ninety-day embargo as a coercive measure (in line with the restrictive system), which undermined the War Hawks' claim that it was a preliminary to war. Moreover, members of both houses showed signs of weariness from the long session and expressed interest in a recess that one Republican claimed would "damp the public spirit and paralyze the energies of the nation." Although the proposed recess was defeated, many members went home anyway.

A Baltimore newspaper circulated a rumor that a special diplomatic mission would be sent to England to avert war. The report, which was widely credited and was repeated as far away as London, said that Great Britain had offered to resurrect the Monroe-Pinkney Treaty, with certain modifications favorable to the United States, as a basis for preserving peace. With rumors like this afloat, it is hardly surprising that so many people remained skeptical about the prospects for war.

Great Britain, like the United States, was also sending mixed signals, although it was heading in the opposite direction. While the United States was moving toward war, the British were hoping through a series of conciliatory gestures to avert hostilities. The first step in this direction was the settlement of the *Chesapeake* affair in late 1811. After more than four years of sparring, the two powers finally managed to divorce this issue from others and reach a settlement. This problem, however, had festered so long that its resolution gave most Americans little satisfaction.

In the spring of 1812, the British navy began to treat American ships and seamen with new tact. The admiralty ordered all naval officers to take "especial care" to avoid clashes with the American navy and to exercise "all possible forbearance" toward American citizens. The commanding officers at both Halifax and Bermuda ordered their ships to keep clear of the American coast to avoid incidents. This was particularly meaningful because the search and seizure of American ships near the coast was so infuriating.

In May of 1812, on the very eve of war, the British offered to give the United States an equal share of their trade with the European continent, which they had authorized under special licenses. Inasmuch as Britain had issued an average of ten thousand licenses a year since 1807, this proposal was significant. In effect, the British were offering to suspend the Orders in Council in practice if American merchants would conduct their trade with Europe under British licenses. Believing that accepting it would be tantamount to surrendering American independence, the administration summarily rejected this proposal.

The British made their greatest concession in June of 1812, just as the United States was declaring war. On June 16—two days before the declaration of war—Lord Castlereagh, the British foreign secretary, announced in Parliament that the Orders in Council would be suspended. A week later the whole system of blockades and licenses was scrapped. Had there been a transatlantic cable, Castlereagh's announcement might have averted war. Without a speedy means of communication, however, it took weeks for the news to reach the United States, and by then it was too late.

❖ ❖ ❖ ❖ ❖

Although Republican leaders did not realize the British were moving toward peace, they hoped the *Hornet* would bring news of concessions. The long overdue ship finally reached New York on May 19, 1812. Three days later the dispatches it carried were in the hands of officials in Washington. The news, however, was doubly disappointing. Although unofficial reports suggested a softening of British policy, official statements indicated a stubborn adherence to the Orders in Council. The news from France was no better, for in spite of a promise to rescind the Continental Decrees, the French continued to loot American trade. For Americans hoping for concessions from at least one of the belligerents, the *Hornet*'s news was disappointing indeed.

The War Hawks had long since agreed that if the *Hornet* did not bring news of British concessions, they would push for war. Although the Constitution entrusted the decision to Congress, the War Hawks wanted the president to take the lead. Madison did not disappoint them. On June 1, less than ten days after the *Hornet*'s dispatches arrived, he sent a secret message to Congress on the subject of Anglo-American relations.

Madison's message was a well-organized indictment of Great Britain for acts hostile to the United States. The British were arraigned for impressing American seamen; violating American waters; establishing illegal blockades, particularly "the sweeping system of blockades under the name of Orders in Council"; employing a secret agent (John Henry) to subvert the Union; and exerting a malicious influence over the

Indians in the Northwest Territory. The message emphasized maritime issues. Fully two-thirds of the indictment was devoted to the Orders in Council and other blockades.

In places Madison's message echoed the Declaration of Independence, a reflection of the Republican view that a second war of independence was necessary to end Britain's quasi-colonial practices of regulating American trade and impressing American seamen. Fearing the charge of executive influence, Madison did not recommend a declaration of war, but the thrust of his message was unmistakable. "We behold . . . on the side of Great Britain," he said, "a state of war against the United States; and on the side of the United States a state of peace towards Britain."

Madison's message was referred to the House Foreign Relations Committee, which issued a report sharply criticizing Great Britain, particularly for the Orders in Council. Shortly thereafter War Hawk John C. Calhoun introduced a bill declaring war. When the Republicans insisted on debating the measure in secret, the Federalists decided to remain silent. As a result, the Republicans were able to push the bill through the House in only two days—a remarkably short time for so crucial a measure. The final vote on the measure was 79 to 49.

In the Senate the bill ran into more trouble. There was considerable support in this chamber for limiting the war to the high seas. A limited naval war appealed to many people because it offered a direct means of vindicating American rights that was likely to be cheaper than an extended land war. The only problem with this strategy was that the British were far more vulnerable in their sparsely populated Canadian provinces than on the high seas. A maritime war might win some concessions, but it could hardly end in decisive victory.

Although some Republicans (including Monroe and other members of the cabinet) favored a limited maritime war, it was the Federalists who were the most vocal proponents of this strategy. Doubtless recalling the successes of the Quasi-War, the Federalists over the years had repeatedly called for expanding the navy and arming American merchantmen. Most agreed with Josiah Quincy that the nation had a duty to provide "systematic protection of our maritime rights by maritime means." No doubt some Federalists supported maritime war simply as the lesser of two evils—not desirable in itself but preferable to full-scale war. Yet for most, a war restricted to the high seas offered the best means of upholding the nation's rights, especially if (as was widely assumed)

France was included in the reprisals. This would enable Federalist merchants to choose their enemy. Unleashing armed merchantmen against both belligerents, said a Federalist newspaper in Baltimore in a widely reprinted editorial, "meets our peculiar approbation."

The Senate referred the war bill to a select committee, which reported it with little change on June 8. The following day, however, Andrew Gregg, a Republican from Pennsylvania, moved to send the bill back to committee with instructions to amend it so that it merely gave the president authority to permit warships and privateers to make reprisals against Britain. This motion carried by a 17-13 vote. Three days later, however, when the modified bill was reported from committee, the Senate reversed itself. A motion to accept the committee's changes failed by a tie vote, 16 to 16, when President *pro tem* John Gaillard of South Carolina cast his vote against it. The tie vote meant that the original bill was restored.

Although proponents of full-scale war prevailed, the outcome was long in doubt. It took the Senate two weeks to complete its deliberations, which prompted one member of the House to exclaim: "The suspense we are in is worse than hell!!!" Finally, on June 17, the Senate approved the original bill by a 19-13 vote. The following day Madison signed the measure into law. Thus on June 18 the War of 1812 began.

The vote on the war bill—79 to 49 in the House and 19 to 13 in the Senate—was the closest vote on any declaration of war in American history. Only 61 percent of the voting members supported the bill. Most representatives and senators from Pennsylvania and the South and West voted for war, while most from the North and East voted against it. The sectional division was really a reflection of party strength, for the vote on the war bill was essentially a party vote. About 81 percent of the 121 Republicans in both houses of Congress voted for the measure, while all 39 Federalists voted against it.

What did the Republicans hope to accomplish with war? Their chief aim was to win concessions from the British on the maritime issues, particularly the Orders in Council and impressment. Throughout the winter and spring of 1812, these issues had dominated almost every discussion of American grievances, both in and out of Congress. In other words, war was undertaken primarily to secure "free trade and sailors' rights." The advocates of war also hoped to put an end to British influence over American Indians, although this objective was paramount only in the West.

Republicans also saw the struggle as a second war of independence—a contest that would vindicate American sovereignty and preserve republican institutions by demonstrating to the world that the United States could uphold its rights. In addition, the Republicans saw war as a means of preserving power, unifying their party, and silencing their critics. Political considerations loomed large because (like the Federalists in 1798) most Republicans in 1812 identified the interests of their party with those of the nation.

In sum, the Republicans went to war in 1812 to achieve a variety of closely related diplomatic, ideological, and political objectives. The need to take some action was so urgent that Republicans did not wait for their war preparations to mature. This appalled some members of the party, but most were willing to take the risk. In the words of Congressman Robert Wright, they were willing "to get married and buy the furniture afterwards."

For some Republicans—members of the "scarecrow" faction—the risks posed by war did not seem great because they expected the British to cave in to American demands. A Republican senator expressed a common view when he said that the main problem was that the British did not take the threat of war seriously. "I have long since adopted the opinion," said Charles Cutts of New Hampshire, "that if Great Britain would be once convinced that war with this country would be inevitable unless she receded from her unjust pretensions all causes of irritation would be speedily removed." Given the speed with which President Madison later sent out peace feelers, he too might have expected a bloodless victory. In this respect, the declaration of war was a bluff, designed to shock the British into concessions.

The *National Intelligencer* predicted that historians would rank the Twelfth Congress next to "the immortal Congress" of 1776. "Under the auspices of the one this nation sprung into existence; under those of the other it will have been preserved from disgraceful recolonization." Though the comparison with 1776 was exaggerated, it illustrated the ideological legacy of the Revolution, a legacy that most Republicans were unable to shed. For most Republicans, the War of 1812 was very much a second war of independence. But whether the United States could actually vindicate its independence against a foe as powerful as England remained to be seen.

2

THE CAMPAIGN OF 1812

On December 16, 1811, after the debate on the war preparations had been under way for more than two weeks, John Randolph, an anti-war Republican from Virginia, raised a specter that was to haunt contemporaries and historians alike. "Agrarian cupidity," he said, "not maritime right, urges the war. Ever since the report of the Committee on Foreign Relations came into the House, we have heard but one word—like the whip-poor-will, but one eternal monotonous tone—Canada! Canada! Canada!" Randolph exaggerated, since at no time during the debates did territorial expansion overshadow the maritime issues. Although territorial expansionism was a potent force in this era, the desire to conquer and annex Canada did not cause the war. "Canada was not the end but the means," said Henry Clay, "the object of the war being the redress of injuries, and Canada being the instrument by which that redress was to be obtained."

Most Republicans considered British Canada a logical target because it was so weak. About 7.5 million people lived in the United States in 1812, compared with only 500,000 in Canada. The United States had almost 12,000 regulars in uniform, while Canada could muster only 7,000. Additional enlistments, volunteers, and militia drafts were expected to tip the balance still further in favor of the United States, especially since the loyalty of many Canadians was in doubt and Great Britain could ill afford to divert resources from its war in Europe.

What would the United States do with Canada once it was conquered? Since Canada was not an end in itself, presumably it would be held for ransom on the maritime issues. But what if the British balked at concessions? This was a question that Republicans never satisfacto-

rily answered. Although the War Department instructed its commanders in the field to promise Canadians nothing more than protection for
their persons, property, and rights, several senior officers issued proclamations that openly spoke of annexation. The administration's failure to repudiate these proclamations made it all the more difficult to
reconcile domestic opponents of the war.

❖ ❖ ❖ ❖ ❖

In spite of its advantages over Canada, the United States was ill-
equipped to prosecute a major war. The War Department was poorly
organized and understaffed. The work load of the department, heavy
in time of peace, was staggering in time of war. "No man in the country," claimed one War Hawk, "is equal to one-half the duties which
devolve on the present secretary." Although the department had elev-
en clerks, none had more than a year's experience.

The secretary of war, William Eustis, was a good politician, but he
lacked administrative skills and never mastered his duties. Overwhelmed
by the task before him, he frittered away his time on details and failed
to give proper direction to the commanders in the field. "Our secretary
at war," concluded a Pennsylvania Congressman, "is a dead weight in
our hands. . . . His unfitness is apparent to everybody but himself."

Conditions in the army were not much better. The senior officers
were old and incompetent, most owing their appointments to politics.
According to Winfield Scott, "The old officers had, very generally, sunk
into either sloth, ignorance, or habits of intemperate drinking." Though
there were some promising junior officers, many had little military experience. "Our army," complained War Hawk Peter B. Porter in 1813,
"is full of men, fresh from lawyer shops and counting rooms, who know
little of the physical force of man—of the proper means of sustaining
and improving it—or even the mode of its application."

Most of the enlisted men were inexperienced, and morale in the ranks
was low. There were numerous infractions of discipline, and these
multiplied as the army grew. Desertion was so common that less than
four months into the war President Madison felt obliged to issue a
proclamation pardoning all deserters who returned to duty.

Initially the administration planned to rely heavily on short-term
volunteers, but only six regiments were raised during the war, and one
army officer claimed that those he inspected were little better than organized bandits who wasted public property, insulted private citizens,

and freely engaged in "desertion, robbery, [and] disorderly and mutinous conduct." Nor could the militia play the sort of role that Republican leaders envisioned. Except in New England and the West, the militia was poorly equipped and badly organized and had little training. In short, after a decade of neglect, the nation's land forces were not up to fighting a major war.

The system for paying the troops broke down from the beginning. At the start of the war privates earned $5 a month, noncommissioned officers $7 to $9, and officers $20 to $200. To stimulate enlistments, Congress in late 1812 raised the pay of privates and noncommissioned officers by $3. At $8 a month, privates still earned less than the $10 to $12 that unskilled laborers normally made, but steady increases in the enlistment bounty (which ultimately reached $124 and 320 acres of land) pushed army income far above the civilian average.

Even in the first year of the war, when the government had ample resources, administrative inefficiency and slow communication kept many troops from receiving their pay on time. In October 1812 men who had enlisted five months earlier "absolutely refused to march until they had received their pay," and other troops also mutinied for want of pay. As the war progressed, the problem of paying the troops became almost unmanageable. By the fall of 1814 army pay was frequently six to twelve months in arrears, and in some cases even more.

The system of supply was also grossly inefficient. In March of 1812 Congress reestablished the quartermaster and commissary departments (which had been abolished in 1802), but it was months before either department was staffed and operational, and the authority granted to each was vague and overlapping. Throughout the war the supply departments were woefully inefficient, and troops in the field frequently had to go for months without shoes, clothing, blankets, or other vital supplies.

The system for feeding the troops—based on private contract—was even worse. It was "madness in the extreme," said one officer, to rely on such a system in time of war. The daily ration was supposed to consist of 20 ounces of beef or 12 ounces of pork; 18 ounces of bread or flour; 4 ounces of rum, brandy, or whiskey; and small quantities of salt, vinegar, soap, and candles. Contractors and subcontractors, however, were so intent on making a profit that they often delivered bad provisions or chiseled on the quantity.

Complaints over supply multiplied as the war progressed, and many illnesses and deaths were blamed on the system. Doubtless many agreed with General Edmund P. Gaines that "the irregularity in the supply and badness of the rations" had done more than anything else to retard American operations. In fact, one general claimed contractors knocked more men out of combat than the enemy did, and another insisted the men were so badly supplied that the number killed in battle was "trifling" compared with losses from other causes.

The nation had better luck with its ordnance. Congress created a department to supervise this branch of the service on the eve of the war, and it seemed to function smoothly. The nation already had well-established armories at Springfield, Massachusetts, and Harpers Ferry, Virginia, and additional facilities were built during the war. The government was thus able to manufacture and repair small arms, produce ammunition, and test ordnance. The army also purchased cannons and small arms from private firms.

The standard weapon of issue during the war was the .69 caliber smooth-bore musket. This was a muzzle-loaded flintlock that fired a soft lead ball weighing about an ounce. Its effective range was less than a hundred yards, and it misfired 15 percent of the time. Fortunately for the United States, many Americans, particularly in the West, owned rifles. These weapons had a grooved barrel, with a .40 to .60 caliber bore, and an effective range of around two hundred yards. Unlike the fledgling republic during the Revolutionary War, the United States also had ample stocks of powder in 1812.

❖ ❖ ❖ ❖ ❖

Given the state of the War Department and the army, the conquest of Canada was likely to be more difficult than Republicans imagined. Canada in this era was often compared to a tree. The taproots were the sea lanes that stretched across the Atlantic to England; the trunk was the St. Lawrence River; and the outlying communities along the Great Lakes formed the branches. Because the surrounding wilderness was so dense, the western settlements could be supplied only by the water route that followed the river and the lakes. The key to controlling Canada was thus the St. Lawrence, which was dominated by Quebec and Montreal.

There was little enthusiasm for an immediate attack on Quebec because it was heavily fortified and lay north of Federalist New England, which was unlikely to provide the necessary troops and supplies to make the campaign a success. This left Montreal, though an attack on this city would not allow the administration to take advantage of the war enthusiasm in the West or to protect that region from Indian depredations. The president therefore adopted a plan developed by General Henry Dearborn that called for a three-pronged attack against Montreal, the Niagara frontier, and the Detroit frontier.

To manage its operation in the West, the administration chose William Hull, the fifty-nine-year-old governor of Michigan Territory. Hull had a record of distinguished service during the Revolutionary War, but by 1812 he was old and infirm and had lost his taste for battle. In the early summer of 1812 Hull assembled an army of 2,000 regulars and militia in Ohio. His marching orders, which were issued before the declaration of war, called for him to proceed to Fort Detroit, located on the river that linked Lake Erie to Lake Huron.

To facilitate communication, Hull began the laborious task of carving a road out of the wilderness that would link Urbana, Ohio, to Detroit. Arriving at the Maumee (Miami) River at the end of June, he hired the schooner *Cuyahoga* to take his baggage, papers, and supplies to Detroit. Although Hull did not yet know of the declaration of war, the British learned of it in time to seize the ship as it passed by Fort Malden. This enabled them to learn about Hull's plans as well as the size and condition of his army.

Hull reached Detroit on July 5 without further incident. A week later he crossed the Detroit River into British territory with the intention of attacking Fort Malden to the south. Some 200 Ohio militia refused to accompany him, claiming that they could not serve beyond American territory. Hull had to stop to build carriages for his cannons, but otherwise his prospects looked bright. His army was at least twice as large as the British force defending Fort Malden, and a proclamation he issued to the inhabitants induced many Canadian militia to go home or to defect to the United States.

Hull's prospects, however, soon dimmed. The American commander became increasingly worried about his supply lines to Ohio, which were threatened from Lake Erie by the British and from the West by hostile Indians. Although a detachment of 200 militiamen had left Ohio loaded with supplies, they stopped on the Raisin River, some thirty-five miles south of Detroit, and Hull was never able to link up with them. Hull received further bad news at the end of July when he learned that the tiny American outpost on Mackinac (pronounced Mak-i-naw)

Island between Lake Huron and Lake Michigan had surrendered to a large enemy force. Convinced that this "opened the northern hive of Indians" and that "they were swarming down in every direction," Hull decided to withdraw across the river to Detroit, giving up his plan to attack Fort Malden. "This fatal and unaccountable step," said one of his officers, "dispirited the troops" and "left to the tender mercy of the enemy the miserable Canadians who had joined us."

The British made good use of Hull's reprieve. General Isaac Brock had recently arrived with reinforcements, bringing British strength (counting regulars, militia, and Indians) to about 1,600. Brock also knew the condition of the American army from a captured mail bag. "I got possession of the letters my antagonist addressed to the secretary of war," said Brock, "and also of the sentiments which hundreds of his army uttered to their friends. Confidence in the general was gone, and evident despondency prevailed throughout."

Crossing the river, Brock brought his cannons to bear on Fort Detroit and mounted a siege. Playing on Hull's fear of the Indians, he arranged to have a bogus document fall into American hands that mentioned a large body of Indians posed to descend on Detroit. Brock also notified Hull that once the fighting began in earnest he would be unable to control the Indians. With many civilians in the fort (including members of his own family), Hull was horrified by the prospect of an Indian massacre. "My God!" he exclaimed to a subordinate. "What shall I do with these women and children?"

Facing a siege and the possibility of a massacre, Hull became increasingly despondent. Finally, on August 16, 1812, he waved a white flag, surrendering the fort and his entire army. "Not an officer was consulted," reported an observer. "Even the women were indignant at so shameful a degradation of the American character." When Hull later returned to the United States on parole, he was court-martialed and convicted of cowardice and neglect of duty. The court sentenced Hull to death but recommended mercy because of his "revolutionary services and his advanced age." The president approved this verdict and remitted the punishment. Hull and his heirs spent the next thirty-five years trying to vindicate his actions.

Several days before surrendering, Hull had ordered the evacuation of Fort Dearborn in Chicago on the grounds that the fall of Mackinac had rendered its defense untenable. The fort was held by about 65 regulars and militia under the command of Captain Nathan Heald. Some two dozen civilians were also present. The fort was well stocked, the Indians were known to be unfriendly, and almost everyone was opposed to evacuation. Nevertheless, Heald was determined to obey his orders. On August 15 the evacuation was carried out, ostensibly under the protection of 500 Potawatomi Indians. Not far from the fort, the Indians fell on the whites, killing most of them after surrender terms had been arranged. According to one witness, the Indians beheaded one officer, carved out his heart, and ate it raw.

The loss of Mackinac, Detroit, and Dearborn exposed the entire Northwest to enemy attack. The effect of these losses, said the Pittsburgh *Mercury*, was to lay open "to the ravages of the merciless foe the whole extent of our western frontier." Thrown into a panic, westerners bombarded the federal government with demands for protection.

Government officials were anxious to meet these demands and to reestablish American control over the Northwest. Although the administration wanted to assign the western command to General James Winchester, a regular army officer, Kentucky leaders made William Henry Harrison—the hero of Tippecanoe—a major general in the militia and gave him command of all Kentucky troops. This compelled the administration to put Harrison in charge of the whole theater of operations. Harrison spent the fall of 1812 building a huge army that soaked up federal money and supplies at an alarming rate. His intention was to sweep hostile Indians from the region and then retake Detroit, but the onset of winter forced him to give up this plan.

Before ordering his troops into winter quarters, Harrison dispatched a force under Winchester to the rapids of the Maumee River. Following his own councils, Winchester decided to march from the rapids to the Raisin River to protect settlers at Frenchtown (now Monroe, Michigan). Attacked by a force of 1,100 British and Indians, Winchester's troops, which numbered about 850, surrendered on January 22, 1813. Some 300 Americans were killed, including 30 who were massacred by drunken Indians after the surrender had taken place. "The savages *were suffered to commit every depredation upon our wounded,*" reported a group of American officers; "*many were tomahawked, and many were burned alive in the houses.*" Thereafter, "Remember the Raisin!" became a rallying cry throughout the Northwest.

After a season of campaigning in the West, the nation had little to show for the blood and treasure it had expended. Sizable armies had been lost at Detroit and Frenchtown, and forts Mackinac, Detroit, and Dearborn were in enemy hands.

❖ ❖ ❖ ❖ ❖

The campaign in the East did not go much better. The man in charge on the Niagara front was Major General Stephen Van Rensselaer, a forty-eight-year-old Federalist militia officer known as "the last of the patroons." Van Rensselaer had no military experience and relied on his kinsman and aide, Colonel Solomon Van Rensselaer, who had taken part in the Indian wars of the 1790s and had served for many years as adjutant general of New York. The elder Van Rensselaer shared his command in western New York with a regular army officer, General Alexander Smyth. A political appointee, Smyth was without practical experience. Vain and pompous, he refused to place himself under Van Rensselaer's command, despite explicit orders from the War Department to do so.

By October of 1812 there were over 6,000 American troops facing a force of perhaps 2,000 British and Indians across the Niagara River. General Van Rensselaer's plan was to seize Queenston Heights on the British side, while Smyth attacked Fort George six miles to the north. But Smyth, unwilling to take orders from a militia officer, refused to cooperate. Even without Smyth's troops, Van Rensselaer still had a numerical advantage over the British and decided to attack Queenston anyway.

Van Rensselaer planned to send troops across the river on October 11, but this scheme had to be abandoned because, out of either treachery or ignorance, an army officer disappeared down the river in a boat loaded with all the oars. Two days later, another attempt was made. Despite a strong current, an advance guard of some 200 men managed to cross the river. The commanding officer, Solomon Van Rensselaer, was wounded six times in the assault, and his men found themselves pinned down next to the river by British troops occupying the heights above.

Captain John E. Wool took charge of the American force and, discovering an unguarded fisherman's path that led to the heights, marched his men to the top. There the Americans drove off a British force commanded by Brock, who had returned from the West to take charge of the British defenses. Brock was killed in a futile bid to retake the heights, and soon there were about 600 Americans in place, now under the command of Lieutenant Colonel Winfield Scott.

At this point Stephen Van Rensselaer ordered the militia on the American side to cross over to reinforce Scott. But the militiamen, most of whom were said to be "violent Democrats" from New York, were disheartened by the sight of the dead and wounded who were ferried back to the United States. Following the example of their Ohio counterparts in the West, they refused to leave American territory. Without reinforcements, Scott's troops could not resist a fresh assault from the enemy. Driven from the heights, most of the troops—Scott included—surrendered. In all around 950 Americans were captured on the Canadian side of the river.

After this disaster, Van Rensselaer asked to be relieved of his duties, and the War Department, unaware of Smyth's shortcomings, gave him the command. Smyth planned to attack Fort Erie at the south end of the Niagara River, but "Van Bladder" (as his men called him) wasted his time composing bombastic proclamations that even the British found laughable. Sounding more like a postman than a soldier, he told his troops, "Neither rain, snow, or frost will prevent the embarkation." Although a preliminary assault in late November destroyed the enemy's outlying positions at Fort Erie, the primary attack was given up when Smyth's officers voted it down, partly because most of the Pennsylvania militia would not cross the border.

The abandonment of the attack on Fort Erie brought the fighting on the Niagara front to an end. The only thing gained was the death of Brock, a military genius whose loss the Quebec *Gazette* called "a public calamity." As for Smyth, he was bitterly assailed by members of the New York militia, some of whom even took potshots at him. Eventually, using back roads, he stole back to Virginia.

❖　❖　❖　❖　❖

The third and most important thrust in the campaign was supposed to be against Montreal. To head this operation, the administration selected sixty-one-year-old Henry Dearborn, a Revolutionary War veteran who had been Jefferson's secretary of war. Dearborn—known to his troops as "Granny"—had grown fat with prosperity and was no better suited for command than Hull, Van Rensselaer, or Smyth.

Dearborn was so dilatory that the War Department finally had to order him to attack. Still, it was not until November that his army, 6,000 to 8,000 strong, marched from Albany to Plattsburgh on Lake Champlain. A detachment of troops crossed into Canada and skirmished with the British, but the fighting was inconclusive, and in the darkness the Americans fired on each other. Once again the militia, standing on its supposed right to serve only in American territory, refused to cross the border. The whole army soon retreated, and Dearborn gave up this half-hearted attempt on Montreal. A contemporary described his failure as a "miscarriage without even [the] heroism of disaster."

❖ ❖ ❖ ❖ ❖

The American invasion of Canada in 1812 thus failed on all three fronts. The campaign, said a Republican newspaper, had produced nothing but "disaster, defeat, disgrace, and ruin and death." Armies had surrendered at Detroit, Frenchtown, and Queenston; much of the Northwest had fallen into enemy hands; and no headway had been made against British positions on the St. Lawrence.

The principal reason for the failure was poor leadership. The administration's strategy was ill-advised, the War Department failed to give proper direction to commanders in the field, and most of the nation's senior army officers were incompetent. Some of the junior officers, like Winfield Scott and John Wool, had distinguished themselves; and the rank and file had proven adequate, although most were still raw recruits without battlefield experience. As for the militia, it was a major disappointment. When forced to take the offensive, more often than not it had proven undisciplined, unreliable, and unwilling to leave the country.

The entire campaign showed how difficult it was to build an army overnight. "The degraded state in which the military institutions have been retained," concluded the Philadelphia *Aurora*, "comes now upon us with a dismal sentence of retribution."

❖ ❖ ❖ ❖ ❖

The war at sea went much better for the United States in 1812, though not because of superior leadership in the cabinet. The secretary of the navy was Paul Hamilton, a South Carolina rice planter with little knowledge of naval affairs. Hamilton was an alcoholic who was often drunk by noon, and one Republican said that he was "about as fit for his place as the Indian Prophet would be for Emperor of Europe."

A decade of Republican hostility had taken a heavy toll on the navy, but seventeen ships still survived in 1812. Seven were frigates. The *Con-*

stitution, President, and *United States* were rated at 44 guns; the *Constellation, Chesapeake,* and *Congress* at 36 guns; and the *Essex* at 32 guns. Another frigate, the *Adams,* was being cut down to a 28-gun corvette. There were also nine smaller vessels rated at 10 to 20 guns. Most of the ships carried more guns than they were rated for, and most also carried extra crewmen.

The frigates were the heart of the navy. Designed by Philadelphia shipwright Joshua Humphreys, the three heavy frigates—known as "44s"—were longer and sturdier than other frigates. They were capable of carrying heavier guns and were better able to withstand enemy broadsides. In fact, they were "super frigates," capable of outfighting and outsailing other ships in their class and outrunning anything larger.

The nation also had the advantage of a rich maritime tradition. Officers and sailors alike were excellent seamen and skilled marksmen with cannon and small arms. Many had seen action in the Quasi-War (1798–1801) or in the War with Tripoli (1801–5), and some had served on British warships. The morale of the service was high, and the men were trained incessantly to perfect their skills. In addition, the navy did not face the same logistical problems that the army did. The fleet was small, and once supplied a ship could remain at sea for months.

In spite of its high morale, the navy had trouble keeping its ships fully manned. The army siphoned off potential recruits (even some with extensive naval experience) because of the large bounties it offered. The competition from privateers was even greater. Privateering was an attractive alternative to naval service because the tour of duty was short (usually two or three months), the prospect of an armed engagement less, and the chances of large profits greater.

The usual term of service for navy personnel was a year, and normally there was no bounty. The pay ranged from $6 a month for boys and landsmen to $20 for sailmakers. Most could earn more on a merchantman and a lot more on a lucky privateer. To compete, the navy had to offer incentives, including a bounty (ranging from $10 to $30), three months' advance pay, and a 25 percent boost in pay. These incentives went a long way toward securing the men that were needed.

Even when it was fully manned, the tiny American fleet hardly seemed a match for the Mistress of the Seas. For more than a century Great Britain had ruled the waves, and on paper its naval superiority was overwhelming. It had over a thousand ships on the rolls, half of which were at sea at any given time. In 1812, however, the British fleet was scattered all over the world, engaged in patrol, convoy, and blockade duty. Indeed, at the beginning of the war Britain had only one ship-of-the-line, nine frigates, and twenty-seven smaller vessels at its Halifax and Newfoundland stations. There were additional ships attached to its West Indian stations, but many of these were unseaworthy.

❖   ❖   ❖   ❖   ❖

American officials sent the navy to sea in two squadrons (later increased to three) with orders "to afford to our returning commerce all possible protection." But this order arrived after Captain John Rodgers, who was in charge of one of the squadrons, had already set sail in search of a rich British convoy en route from Jamaica to England. Although he never caught up with the convoy, Rodgers's cruise had a dramatic effect on British naval strategy.

Vice Admiral Herbert Sawyer, commander of the Halifax station, had planned to post a British cruiser in front of each American port to intercept returning merchantmen. When he learned that Rodgers was at sea with a large squadron, however, he gave up this plan, fearing that his vessels might be picked off one at a time. Instead, Sawyer kept his fleet concentrated and spent most of his time searching for Rodgers's squadron. As a result, he was able to make only one sweep through American waters, and his catch was poor. "We have been so completely occupied looking for Commodore Rodgers's squadron," a British officer complained, "that we have taken very few prizes."

Because the British did not patrol American waters, most American merchant vessels were able to reach home safely. The windfall for the United States was considerable. The flood of goods replenished the nation's stocks and buoyed the customs revenue. In addition, returning seamen helped fill out the crews of American warships and privateers that were fitting out for sea.

Some American warships cruised separately in 1812, and their record of accomplishments was impressive. Captain Isaac Hull, the nephew of the disgraced army general, commanded the USS *Constitution,* the nation's best frigate. After putting on a magnificent show of seamanship by outrunning a British squadron, Hull took on supplies in Boston and set sail again.

On August 19, about 750 miles east of Boston, the *Constitution* (which carried 54 guns) encountered HMS *Guerrière* (with 49 guns), a ship that was commanded by Captain James R. Dacres and was described by the British *Naval Chronicle* as "one of our stoutest frigates." After outmaneuvering the enemy, Hull's ship delivered a powerful and destructive raking fire. An American on board the British ship said the *Constitution's* double-shotted first fire (700 pounds of metal delivered at close range) sounded like "a tremendous explosion" and forced the *Guerrière* to "reel and tremble as though she had received the shock of an earthquake."

Although the *Guerrière* returned the fire, its masts were soon destroyed, its hull damaged, and most of its crew knocked out of action. This left Dacres with no choice but to surrender. Unable to salvage the British ship, Hull removed its crew and ordered it set on fire and sent to the bottom. During the battle, a seaman on the *Constitution* had seen round shot bounce off the ship and had exclaimed, "Huzza! Her sides are made of iron." Thereafter, the *Constitution* was affectionately known as "Ironsides" or "Old Ironsides."

On October 15 the USS *United States*, a 56-gun frigate commanded by Stephen Decatur, was cruising six hundred miles west of the Canaries when it encountered a British frigate, HMS *Macedonian* (49 guns), commanded by Captain John S. Carden. Although the *United States* was known as "the Wagon" because it was such a poor sailer, Decatur outmaneuvered his foe, keeping his distance to take advantage of his powerful long-range guns and his crew's marksmanship. In the ensuing battle, the *United States* got off seventy broadsides, the *Macedonian* only thirty. A seaman on the British ship described the damage done by the American guns: "Grapeshot and canister were pouring through our portholes like leaden hail; the large shot came against the ship's side, shaking her to the very keel, and passing through her timbers and scattering terrific splinters, which did more appalling work than the shot itself."

By the time the *Macedonian* got close enough to the *United States* to use its guns effectively, it had lost most of its spars and rigging and a third of its crew, forcing Carden to strike his colors. When Decatur boarded the vessel, he found "fragments of the dead scattered in every direction, the decks slippery with blood, [and] one continuous agonizing yell of the unhappy wounded." A prize crew sailed the *Macedonian* into Newport Harbor, the only time a British frigate has ever been brought into an American port as a prize of war.

Another American victory followed off the coast of Brazil on December 29, 1812, when the *Constitution*, now commanded by William

Bainbridge, met HMS *Java* (49 guns), a frigate under the command of Captain Henry Lambert. Both captains demonstrated excellent seamanship, but once again superior firepower and marksmanship carried the day for the United States. American gunners destroyed most of the *Java*'s rigging and killed or wounded a large portion of the British crew. Unable to maneuver, the *Java* surrendered. After removing the crew and passengers, Bainbridge sent the British hulk to the bottom.

Several smaller American ships also distinguished themselves. The USS *Wasp* (18 guns) defeated HMS *Frolic* (16 guns), the USS *Hornet* (18 guns) beat the British sloop *Peacock* (18 guns), and the small American frigate *Essex* (which was overloaded with 46 guns) defeated the British brig *Alert* (20 guns). Although the British captured three American warships—the *Wasp*, *Nautilus* (14 guns), and *Vixen* (14 guns)—the balance was clearly in favor of the United States.

In all, the United States had defeated three British frigates and four smaller vessels while losing only three small vessels of its own. American success was due not only to the superior firepower of the heavy frigates but also to the skillful seamanship and gunnery displayed on all the ships.

The American navy also captured fifty enemy merchant vessels, but the real damage to British commerce in 1812 was done by American privateers—sometimes called "the militia of the sea." Although British warships in the New World captured more than 150 privateers in the first eight months of the war, armed American vessels took 450 prizes in the first six months. "*Jonathan*'s privateers," complained a correspondent to the British *Naval Chronicle*, "have roved with impunity and success to all corners of the earth."

❖ ❖ ❖ ❖ ❖

The war at sea gave a tremendous boost to American morale, a boost that was sorely needed because the nation was reeling from the disasters on the Canadian frontier. "Our brilliant naval victories," said an army officer, "serve, in some measure, to wipe out the disgrace brought upon the nation by the conduct of our generals." There was also considerable pride in humbling the Mistress of the Seas in its own element. "British arms cannot withstand American upon the sea," exulted a Republican Congressman. "The bully has been disgraced by an infant."

The British, on the other hand, were stunned by their losses. In more than two hundred naval engagements with France and its allies over a twenty-year period, the British had lost only five battles. Some British subjects, like the editor of the *Times*, acknowledged the merits of American ships and sailors, but most shared the view of the London *Evening Star*, which described the American navy as "a few fir-built frigates, manned by a handful of bastards and outlaws." Given this contempt, the American victories went down hard. "It is a cruel mortification," said a cabinet official, "to be beat by these secondhand Englishmen upon our own element."

In response to growing criticism, the British government dispatched additional ships to the New World and launched a crash program to build heavy frigates. In addition, the admiralty secretly ordered British frigates not to cruise alone or "to engage, single-handed, the larger class of American ships, which, though they may be called frigates . . . [resemble] line-of-battle ships." The government also ordered all merchantmen in the Atlantic to sail in convoy.

❖ ❖ ❖ ❖ ❖

The outcome of the campaign of 1812 was a surprise to people on both sides of the Atlantic. The conquest of Canada, which was supposed to be (in Jefferson's words) a "mere matter of marching," had eluded the United States, while the war at sea, in which the British were supposed to have a decisive advantage, had gone surprisingly well for the United States. Both sides had been unprepared for the war, which had worked to Britain's advantage in Canada but to America's on the high seas.

Time, however, was on Great Britain's side. In June of 1812 Napoleon had taken the largest army ever assembled, some 600,000 men, into Russia. By the fall of 1812 stout resistance and a lack of supplies had forced him to retreat. The retreat soon turned into a rout, and by the end of the year the Grand Army had melted away. If Napoleon's fortunes continued to wane, England would be able to concentrate its military and naval might against the United States, and there would be little chance for the young Republic to take Canada or to win any maritime concessions. For the United States, in other words, time was running out.

3

THE CAMPAIGN OF 1813

When the spring thaw opened the campaigning season in 1813, the United States was in a stronger position than it had been in 1812. John Armstrong had replaced William Eustis as secretary of war, and William Jones had taken over for Paul Hamilton as secretary of the navy. Although Armstrong was despised by everyone else in the cabinet, these changes improved the nation's leadership in Washington.

There was also better leadership in the field. William Henry Harrison and Andrew Jackson were emerging in the West, and young officers, such as Winfield Scott, were making their marks on the northern frontier. In addition, the troops in the line were better. Although enlistments lagged behind need, the combination of better pay and higher bounties had attracted large numbers to the service. By the spring of 1813, there were about 30,000 men in uniform—more than twice as many as there were when the war began. Although most of the troops were still inexperienced, the campaign of 1812 had turned some into seasoned veterans.

❖ ❖ ❖ ❖ ❖

American strategy in 1813 once again focused on targets in Upper Canada. Quebec was ignored because it was so heavily fortified, and even Montreal was considered too well defended to be a primary target. Instead, the administration's plan—which was developed by Armstrong—called for attacking Kingston (Britain's principal naval base on Lake Ontario), then York (a secondary naval base), and finally Fort George and Fort Erie (which anchored the enemy's defenses on the

Niagara River). Success against these targets was expected to pave the way for operations against other British strongholds.

The key to the campaign was control of the Great Lakes—particularly Ontario and Erie. Because of the dense wilderness and lack of good roads, the lakes offered the only efficient means of moving men and materiel along the northern frontier. Whoever controlled the lakes controlled the whole border region.

At the beginning of the war, the British held undisputed sway over both lakes, and this played a central role in Brock's success in 1812. While Hull had to supply and reinforce his troops by using undeveloped and exposed roads, Brock was able to use Lake Erie. This enabled him to capture Detroit while still maintaining effective resistance along the Niagara frontier.

American officials were aware of the importance of controlling the lakes but had hoped that a few well-aimed strokes would destroy British power in Canada and render the whole question academic. It was only after Hull's defeat that the administration resolved to secure command of the lakes. Accordingly, in September of 1812 the administration ordered Captain Isaac Chauncey, a forty-year-old veteran naval officer, "to assume command of the naval force on lakes Erie and Ontario, and to use every exertion to obtain control of them this fall."

The nation already had a naval base at Sackets Harbor, New York, on Lake Ontario, and Chauncey now chose Presque Isle (which is now Erie, Pennsylvania) for his base on Lake Erie. By purchasing merchant vessels and converting them into small warships, and by launching an energetic program to build larger ones, Chauncey hoped to wrest control of the lakes from the British.

British officials fully appreciated the significance of Chauncey's challenge but found it difficult to match America's building program because they had to ship most of their naval equipment across the Atlantic and then over a Canadian water route that was both long and exposed. Moreover, the British waited until March of 1813 to put a competent navy officer, Sir James Yeo, in charge of their forces on the lakes.

There was little action on Lake Ontario in the early months of the war, but by the end of 1812 the United States had enough ships to challenge the British for control. Thereafter the balance of power tipped back and forth between the two nations, depending on the progress of their building programs and the deployment of their ships. Because both commanders—Chauncey and Yeo—were cautious, there was no decisive fleet action, though each tried to destroy the other's naval base.

Although American strategy called for attacking Kingston first, Dearborn and Chauncey persuaded Armstrong to substitute York (present-day Toronto). In late April 1813 Chauncey departed from Sackets Harbor with a force of 1,700 troops under the command of General Zebulon Pike, a capable young officer who had already gained fame as an explorer. On April 27 the American force landed west of York, which was defended by 700 British and Indians under the command of General Sir Roger Sheaffe. Supported by Chauncey's fleet (which had to fight gale-force winds), Pike's army attacked the town and overwhelmed its defenders, forcing Sheaffe to retreat to the interior.

The British suffered 150 killed and wounded and 290 captured in the Battle of York. The Americans sustained 320 casualties, most of which were caused by the explosion of the garrison's magazine. The blast caused so many injuries that army doctors waded "in blood, cutting off arms [and] legs and trepanning [boring holes in] heads." Among the casualties was General Pike, who was killed when "a large stone struck him in the forehead and stamped him for the grave."

American soldiers, already angry over the explosion, found a scalp in one of the government buildings in York and used this as an excuse to loot the town. They were joined by British subjects who had come in from the countryside. "Every house they found deserted was completely sacked," said a local resident. The Americans also torched the government buildings. The British later used this to justify burning Washington.

Despite the heavy toll, the capture of York was an important victory. The United States seized one British ship, and the British destroyed another as well as a large quantity of naval stores. This helped the United States maintain parity on Lake Ontario and hampered British operations on Lake Erie.

The British responded in May of 1813 by attacking Sackets Harbor. At dawn on May 29 Commodore Yeo's fleet landed 750 troops under the command of Colonel Edward Baynes on the American shore. The base was defended by 400 regulars and 500 militia under General Jacob Brown of the New York militia. Although the militia soon fled, the regulars held fast, pouring on a steady stream of fire that forced the British to withdraw. The British suffered 260 killed, wounded, and missing, while American losses were only about 100.

❖ ❖ ❖ ❖ ❖

Although there was no decisive operation on Lake Ontario in 1813, the action on Lake Erie was quite different. When Chauncey assumed command of the lakes in the fall of 1812, he dispatched Lieutenant Jesse Elliott to Lake Erie to build and buy ships suitable for naval service.

In an imaginative night raid, Elliott attacked two British schooners fitting out on the Niagara River near Buffalo, burning the *Detroit*, mounting 6 guns, and then capturing the *Caledonia*, a private armed vessel mounting 2 guns. The loss of these vessels and the supplies they carried—the hold of the *Detroit* was loaded with ordnance captured at Detroit—was a serious blow to the British.

At the end of 1812 Chauncey put twenty-seven-year-old Oliver H. Perry in charge of Lake Erie. Arriving at Presque Isle in the spring of 1813, Perry worked at a frantic pace to complete four ships that were under construction there. To these he added five vessels stationed on the Niagara River—the *Caledonia* and four merchantmen purchased by Elliott.

With a ragtag crew that consisted of many landsmen, Perry took command of the *Lawrence* (20 guns) and assigned the *Niagara* (20 guns) to Lieutenant Elliott. The fleet of nine vessels then set sail for Put-in-Bay, which was located in the Bass Islands at the western end of the lake. This afforded a good vantage point for watching the British fleet, which was anchored at Amherstburg.

The commander of the British squadron was Captain Robert H. Barclay, an experienced naval officer who had served with Lord Nelson at Trafalgar and had lost an arm in the service (which prompted Indians to call him "our father with one arm"). Barclay's fleet of six ships was inferior to Perry's force, especially at close range. Like Perry, Barclay faced a manpower shortage that could be remedied only by using soldiers. He was also short of provisions because the British army was trying to feed a large number of Indians at Amherstburg. Goaded on by the army, Barclay decided "to risk everything" to open his lines of communication. Accordingly, he sallied forth to meet Perry's fleet.

On September 10, 1813, the opposing squadrons came within sight of each other. The Americans had the weather gage (the wind at their backs). According to Barclay, this was "a prodigious advantage" because it enabled Perry to choose his distance. The British opened fire at long range, which was their best strategy, but Perry soon ordered his ships to move in to take full advantage of his fire power. Elliott, however, held the *Niagara* back, preferring for reasons that have never been satisfactorily explained to rely on his long guns. This meant that Perry fought the British ships at close range with only minimal assistance from his second largest ship.

The *Lawrence* repeatedly traded broadsides with the two largest British ships, the *Detroit* (21 guns), which was Barclay's flagship, and the *Queen Charlotte* (18 guns). The fire was so intense that a British marine who had been at Trafalgar claimed that "that was a mere fleabite in comparison with this." After two hours of fighting, all three ships were severely damaged. Perry's crew had suffered more than 80 percent casualties, forcing the commodore to call up the wounded from below to aid in the fight.

When his ship had become a floating hulk, Perry hopped into a small boat manned by several sailors and rowed to the *Niagara*, miraculously escaping injury from the rain of fire around him. Taking command of the *Niagara*, he sailed back into the heart of the British fleet, this time exchanging fire with three ships on each side. When the *Detroit* and *Queen Charlotte* became fouled, they were shot to pieces by the *Niagara* and two American schooners.

Three hours into the battle, the larger British ships had been destroyed, and the first and second in command on all six British vessels had been killed or wounded. Barclay himself had to be carried below, his good arm now mangled. Four of the British ships struck their colors. Two others tried to escape but were run down and forced to surrender too.

Perry's triumph on Lake Erie was a tribute to his courage and coolness under fire and to the effective use of his superior resources. On the back of an old letter he wrote a note to Harrison that added even more luster to his name: "We have met the enemy and they are ours: two ships, two brigs, one schooner, and one sloop." The American victory was the most important on the Great Lakes during the war. It changed the balance of power in the West and enabled the United States to recover all that it had lost in 1812.

❖ ❖ ❖ ❖ ❖

By the time Perry's victory had secured Lake Erie, the campaign in the Northwest was already under way, for the British had taken the offensive in the spring of 1813. Prodded by Tecumseh and his followers, General Henry Procter assembled an army of 900 regulars and militia and 1,200 Indians to attack Fort Meigs (in Ohio), which was defended by only 550 men under Harrison. The Americans held out, and Procter withdrew, though not before mauling a 1,200-man relief force that had arrived from Kentucky.

After the battle, the Indians massacred some of the prisoners. Tecumseh was appalled by Procter's inability to halt this slaughter. "Begone!" he reportedly exclaimed, "you are unfit to command; go and put on petticoats." In all, the United States suffered 320 killed and wounded and 600 captured. British losses (excluding Indians) were only about 100.

In late July Procter invaded Ohio again, this time with a force of 5,000 regulars, militia, and Indians. Following a plan developed by Tecumseh, the British hoped to lure the defenders out of Fort Meigs by staging a sham battle nearby. When this plan failed, Procter detached 400 troops and a large body of Indians for an assault on Fort Stephenson on the Sandusky River, which was defended by 160 men under twenty-one-year-old Major George Croghan. When the British reached a ditch at the edge of the fort, they were cut down by Kentucky sharpshooters and a concealed cannon. Calling this "the severest fire I ever saw," Procter gave up the attack and ordered his troops back to Canada. He blamed the defeat on the Indians, who had clamored for action and then disappeared when the fighting began.

The attack on Fort Stephenson was the last British offensive in the Northwest, for the following month Perry's victory deprived them of control of Lake Erie. Unable to secure supplies by water, Procter decided to withdraw to the interior via the Thames River. Tecumseh bitterly assailed this decision and publicly compared Procter to "a fat animal that carries its tail upon its back but when affrighted . . . drops it between his legs and runs off." The only concession he could win from the British general was a promise to make a stand somewhere on the Thames.

While Perry repaired his fleet so it could be used to transport men and supplies, Harrison raised additional troops, mostly in Kentucky, including 1,200 highly trained mounted volunteers under the command of Congressman Richard M. Johnson. This brought American strength to about 5,500 men.

The Americans occupied Detroit and Malden, which the British had abandoned in their flight to the interior. Although 150 Pennsylvania militia refused to cross the border, the Kentucky militia had no such qualms. Most of Harrison's army crossed into Canada, and the pursuit of Procter began in earnest. Procter moved at a leisurely pace and failed to destroy all the bridges behind him. The Americans soon came across baggage and supplies discarded by the British. They also captured two gunboats on the Thames that contained Procter's spare ammunition.

With the Americans closing in, Procter decided to make a stand near Moraviantown, about fifty miles east of Detroit. Procter's force consisted of over 800 regulars and 500 Indians. The men were arrayed in open order in two thin lines extending from the river to a large swamp. Harrison approached on October 5 with 3,000 men, including Johnson's regiment. Finding the British lines thin, Johnson asked for permission to make a frontal assault with his mounted troops. Although a cavalry charge like this was extremely unorthodox, Harrison consented to the plan.

Shouting "Remember the Raisin!" Johnson's troops galloped toward the enemy. The right wing easily burst through the British line and then dismounted and caught the British in a cross fire, forcing them to surrender. The Indians continued their resistance longer, but when word spread that Tecumseh had been killed, most of them fled. Johnson (who suffered several disabling wounds in the engagement) was credited with killing Tecumseh, which helped catapult him into the vice presidency in 1836. The Americans took clothing, hair, and even patches of skin from Tecumseh's body for souvenirs. "I [helped] kill Tecumseh and [helped] skin him," a veteran of the campaign recalled a half-century later, "and brought two pieces of his yellow hide home with me to my mother and sweethearts."

The Battle of the Thames was a great victory for the United States. Although the casualties on both sides were light, the Americans captured 600 British soldiers as well as a large quantity of war materiel. Coupled with Perry's victory, the battle turned the tide in the West and secured the whole region for the United States. As proof of the new state of affairs, some of the hostile Indian tribes signed a treaty with the United States that bound them to wage war against Britain.

❖ ❖ ❖ ❖ ❖

The campaign along the Niagara front also had a promising start, but in the end reverses and mismanagement cost the United States all that it had gained. The principal target of American troops here was Fort

George, located on the Canadian side where the Niagara River flows into Lake Ontario. The British fort was garrisoned by 1,100 regulars and militia, under the command of General John Vincent.

In May of 1813 the United States assembled a force of 4,500 troops across from Fort George. On May 24 American artillery units opened fire on Newark, a small town near Fort George that housed some of the British soldiers. Three days later Chauncey laid down an artillery barrage from the lake to cover a landing of American troops west of the fort. The landing—a joint operation directed by Winfield Scott and Commodore Perry—put American troops in the position to attack the fort from the rear. The British came out to meet the invaders but were outgunned and outnumbered. Forced to give ground, they abandoned the fort and fled south. Scott pursued the British but was ordered to return to Fort George by General Morgan Lewis, who was temporarily in command. The British lost 350 killed, wounded, and captured in the Battle of Fort George, compared with American losses of only 140.

Since the loss of this fort exposed British positions all along the Niagara frontier, Vincent ordered the evacuation of the other British garrisons—Fort Chippewa, Queenston, and Fort Erie—each of which was subsequently occupied by American troops. The United States now controlled the entire frontier, but its failure to follow up on this initial victory proved costly, for Vincent was able to regroup his forces at Burlington Heights (now Hamilton).

After reforming his army, Vincent defeated American forces at Stoney Creek and Beaver Dams. He then launched a series of predatory raids across the Niagara River in the hope of forcing the Americans to evacuate Fort George. This strategy worked. Most American regulars had been transferred east, leaving only 250 men to defend the entire frontier. Attempts to call out New York militia failed because everyone knew that the pay was in arrears and that even though winter was at hand the only housing available was tents. Few of the militia were willing to serve in Canada anyway. Under these circumstances, the commanding officer, General George McClure of the New York militia, decided to abandon Fort George on December 10, 1813, though before doing so he burned Newark to deny British troops shelter there. The inhabitants were given only twelve hours' notice in subzero temperatures to vacate their homes.

General Sir Gordon Drummond, who had assumed command of the British forces in this theater of operations, was furious over the callous treatment of Newark's civilians and authorized retaliation. On December 18 a British force of 550 men surprised the American sentries at Fort Niagara (across the river from Fort George), extracted the password, and then secured access to the fort. The American commander of the post was reportedly drunk at his home three miles away, and no one in the fort had taken any precautions. "Our men," said General McClure, "were nearly all asleep in their tents; the enemy rushed in and commenced a most horrid slaughter." The British inflicted 80 casualties (mostly by bayonet) and took 350 prisoners, while suffering fewer than a dozen casualties themselves.

Another British force under General Phineas Riall crossed into American territory on December 18 and destroyed Lewiston as well as two smaller towns nearby. The Indians who accompanied Riall got drunk and left a ghastly scene at Lewiston. According to an American who later visited the town, "The sight we here witnessed was shocking beyond description. Our neighbors were seen lying dead in the fields and roads, some horribly cut and mangled with tomahawks, others eaten by the hogs." The British also burned Black Rock and Buffalo. "The whole frontier from Lake Ontario to Lake Erie," lamented Governor Daniel Tompkins of New York, "is depopulated and the buildings and improvements, with a few exceptions, destroyed."

❖ ❖ ❖ ❖ ❖

The reason the Niagara frontier was so exposed in the second half of 1813 was that most of the regulars stationed there had been sent east for service on the St. Lawrence River front. Several things, however, doomed the eastern campaign to failure. The War Department did not decide to mount this campaign until the season was well advanced; the United States lost an important supply route when the British won control of Lake Champlain by capturing two American ships; and the American commander in this theater, General James Wilkinson, was incompetent and corrupt.

The plan of operations was vague, but ultimately Montreal was the target. Wilkinson was supposed to lead 7,000 men from Sackets Harbor down the St. Lawrence River and approach Montreal from the west, while Wade Hampton (who despised Wilkinson and refused to take orders from him) was to approach with 4,500 men from the south. The campaign did not get under way until October, and neither commanding officer showed much confidence in the plan or much interest in cooperating.

Hampton launched his invasion by following the Chateaugay River, which empties into the St. Lawrence not far from Montreal. Most of Hampton's militia (about 1,000 men) refused to cross the border, and even the regulars, most of whom were raw recruits, were undependable. To repel Hampton's invasion, Lieutenant Colonel Charles de Salaberry organized 1,400 French Canadian militia behind extremely strong defensive works.

The Battle of Chateaugay took place on October 26. Unable to get any of his troops around the Canadian position for an attack from the rear, Hampton ordered a frontal assault. But de Salaberry's troops raised such a din with shouting and bugles that the Americans fell back, convinced that they faced a huge army. Actual casualties on both sides were light, but Hampton gave up the invasion and returned to the United States.

Wilkinson proved no more eager to carry out his part of the operation. He wanted the administration to order the attack (so he could avoid blame if it failed), and he did not begin his descent down the St. Lawrence until November 5. From the beginning, he was hampered by problems: personal illness, bad weather, and harassment from Colonel Joseph Morrison's 800-man force to his rear.

When Wilkinson reached Chrysler's Farm, he determined to crush Morrison's force, but since he was too ill to conduct the operation himself, he put General John P. Boyd in charge of 2,000 troops to accomplish the task. Boyd attacked on November 11 but could not dislodge the British regulars from their positions. Despite their inferior numbers, the British drove the Americans from the field with a counterattack. British casualties in the Battle of Chrysler's Farm were about 180, while the Americans lost 340 killed and wounded and 100 captured. With this defeat, Wilkinson called off the campaign and went into winter quarters.

❖ ❖ ❖ ❖ ❖

There was also fighting on the southern frontier in 1813, though here the Creek Indians fought alone, without any assistance from the British. The Creeks occupied most of present-day Alabama and were loosely allied with neighboring tribes in a large confederation. Like Indians elsewhere in the West, they had long been nursing grievances against Americans for encroaching on their lands.

Tecumseh had visited the tribe in 1811, hoping to persuade the Creeks to return to their traditional ways and join his crusade against whites. Although the older chiefs withstood Tecumseh's entreaties, a young faction—known as the Red Sticks—was more receptive. The Red Sticks were emboldened by the Anglo-Indian victories in the Northwest and by promises of aid from Spanish officials in Florida.

A small band of Red Sticks traveled to the Northwest to visit Tecumseh in 1812. These Indians took part in the River Raisin massacre at the beginning of 1813 and departed for home filled with hatred for Americans and with visions of rolling back white settlements all along the frontier. When they reached the mouth of the Duck River south of Nashville in Tennessee, they murdered several white people living there. To keep peace with the whites, the old Creek chiefs ordered the guilty Indians hunted down and killed. This precipitated a civil war in the tribe, and most of the old chiefs had to flee to the American Indian agent for protection. With the Red Sticks in the ascendant, Indian raids in the Southwest increased.

In July of 1813 a group of Red Sticks visited Pensacola to trade for European goods and to pick up arms promised by Spanish officials. On July 27, as the Indians were returning with their pack train, they were attacked eighty miles north of Pensacola by 180 Mississippi militia. In the skirmishing that followed—known as the Battle of Burnt Corn—the Americans ended up with most of the supplies, but they were driven from the field, which further emboldened the Indians. This was the opening battle in the Creek War. It transformed what had been a civil war in the Creek Confederation into a larger war with the United States.

The Creeks retaliated on August 30 by attacking Fort Mims, a stockade forty miles north of Mobile. The fort was occupied by 300 people, including 120 militia, under the command of Major Daniel Beasley, a regular army officer. Beasley took his duties lightly and did not adequately prepare the fort for defense. Ignoring a warning from slaves who had spotted Indians earlier in the day, the Americans were caught by surprise and overwhelmed. The Indian assailants paid dearly, losing at least 100 killed and many more wounded, but they killed close to 250 of the defenders, including many women and children.

Early reports greatly exaggerated the number of people killed at Fort Mims and "spread consternation through the territory." The Fort Mims massacre stirred up people in the Southwest, much as the River Raisin massacre had galvanized people in the Northwest. Expeditions against the Indians were mounted from Georgia and the Mississippi Territory. Although these campaigns took a heavy toll on the Indians, the results were inconclusive.

People in Tennessee also responded to the call for action. Although the heart of the Creek country was least accessible from this state, by the fall of 1813 some 2,500 militia had gathered for a punitive expedition under the leadership of Andrew Jackson, a major general in the Tennessee militia. A tough Indian-fighter who was already known as "Old Hickory," Jackson planned to wipe out the hostile Indians and then seize Spanish Florida.

Marching rapidly south, Jackson built Fort Strother on the Coosa River to serve as a forward base for his operations. On November 3 his most able lieutenant, General John Coffee, attacked an Indian village at Tallushatchee. Using tactics employed by Hannibal two thousand years earlier, Coffee formed his men into a semicircle around the village, induced the Indians to attack, and then closed the loop. Coffee sustained fewer than 50 casualties in the Battle of Tallushatchee, while the Indians suffered at least 200 killed and 84 women and children captured.

Several days later Jackson learned that 1,100 hostile Creeks were besieging a town of friendly Indians at Talladega. Jackson marched 2,000 men to the town and on November 9 used the same tactics as Coffee's to envelop the hostile Indians. This time, however, the Indians found a weak spot in the line and managed to break through and escape. The Battle of Talladega was nonetheless an American victory, for the Indians left 300 dead on the field while Jackson's losses were only about 100.

At this point, Jackson had to suspend operations and return to Fort Strother because his provisions were low. Like so many generals in this war, Jackson had to contend with recurring problems with his contractors. In addition, many of his troops, whose terms of service had expired, wanted to go home. On several occasions Jackson had to threaten volunteers with militia or militia with volunteers in order to keep his army intact. It was only by sheer force of will that the Tennessee general kept his army together and the campaign alive.

Ultimately Jackson had to permit most of his troops to go home. But by early 1814 reinforcements had arrived, raising his strength to 1,000 men. Resuming the offensive, Jackson marched into the very heart of Creek country, where he fought two engagements: one at Emuckfau on January 22 and the other at Enotachopco Creek two days later. The fighting in both battles was intense, but each time the outcome was inconclusive. Jackson sustained about a hundred casualties, while the Indians probably lost twice this number.

After returning again to Fort Strother, Jackson stockpiled supplies and waited for fresh troops. Tales of his campaign stimulated recruiting in Tennessee, and by February of 1814 his army was 4,000 strong. Among the new arrivals were 600 regulars. Jackson hoped that these troops would "give strength to [his] arm and quell mutiny," but he continued to have trouble with the militia. When one young soldier, John Woods, refused to obey orders, Jackson ordered him court-martialed. The defendant was convicted and shot—the first execution of a militiaman since the Revolution. The sanguinary lesson was not lost on Jackson's men. In this campaign, as in others, Jackson got the most out of his men because they feared him more than they feared the enemy.

Jackson learned from friendly Indians that about 1,000 hostile Creeks had established themselves on a peninsula called Horseshoe Bend on the Tallapoosa River. The Indians had fortified the land approach and placed their canoes on the river in case they had to flee. Jackson marched to the scene with about 3,000 men and carefully laid plans for an attack.

The battle began on March 27, 1814, when Jackson began pounding the enemy's breastworks with two small fieldpieces. At the same time, friendly Indians in the rear swam across the river and made off with the Creeks' canoes. Next, a detachment of Indians and whites again crossed the river and attacked the Creeks from the rear. Shortly thereafter, Jackson ordered his own troops to storm the Creeks' defenses. The breastworks were soon breached, and a disorganized battle followed that raged well into the night and then resumed the next morning. The Battle of Horseshoe Bend was a slaughter because most of the Creeks preferred death to surrender and those who tried to escape were shot down. Even Jackson admitted that the "*carnage* was *dreadful.*" Close to 800 hostile Indians perished, while Jackson's own force sustained only 200 casualties.

Even though many of the Creeks had sided with the United States, on August 9, 1814, Jackson forced all the tribal leaders to sign the Treaty of Fort Jackson, which stripped the Indians of more than 20 million acres of land—over half of their territory. Such a massive land grab pleased Jackson's western supporters but left officials in Washington aghast.

Jackson's victories in the Southwest, coupled with those of Perry and Harrison in the Northwest, greatly increased American security on the western frontier. The only problem with these victories was that they had occurred in regions too remote to have a decisive effect on the outcome of the war. On the more important fronts—along the Niagara and St. Lawrence rivers—the United States had made no headway in its efforts to dislodge the British. After two years of campaigning, Canada still remained in British hands, and victory seemed as remote as ever.

❖ ❖ ❖ ❖ ❖

If the war on land went better for the United States in 1813, the war at sea went worse. This was to be expected because the ocean was Britain's element. The British had been slow to exploit their naval superiority in the first six months of the war, which had led to considerable domestic criticism. In response, the government in early 1813 increased its naval force in American waters to 10 ships-of-the-line, 38 frigates, and 52 smaller vessels.

Sir John Borlase Warren, who was put in charge of British naval forces in the North Atlantic, had already established a blockade from Charleston, South Carolina, to Spanish Florida in the fall of 1812. He extended this blockade in December to the Chesapeake and Delaware bays and then, when his fleet was enlarged in 1813, to other ports and harbors in the middle and southern states. By November 1813 the entire coast south of New England was under blockade. Warren exempted New England from the blockade, both to reward it for opposing the war and to keep up the flow of provisions from that region to Canada and the British West Indies.

The British blockade had a deadly effect on the United States. Foreign trade dropped sharply, and government revenue dried up. "Commerce is becoming very slack," reported a resident of Baltimore in the spring of 1813; "no arrivals from abroad, and nothing going to sea but sharp [fast] vessels." By the end of the year, the sea lanes had become so dangerous that insurance for ocean-going vessels had soared to 50 percent of the value of the ship and cargo.

With British warships hovering nearby, the coastal trade also had become perilous, forcing American merchants to resort to overland transportation. There were few good roads, however, and even the best broke down under heavy use and the ongoing assault of the elements. "The roads [in Virginia] . . . are worse than usual," Nathaniel Macon reported in March of 1813; "it takes 38 hours to travel from Fredericksburg to Alexandria, the distance 50 miles."

The lack of good transportation created gluts and shortages throughout the American economy. Sugar that sold for $9 a hundredweight in August of 1813 in New Orleans commanded $21.50 in New York and $26.50 in Baltimore. Rice selling for $3 a hundredweight in Charleston or Savannah brought $9 in New York and $12 in Philadelphia. And flour, which was $4.50 a barrel in Richmond, went for $8.50 in New York and almost $12 in Boston.

The British used their naval power not only to put economic pressure on the United States but also to bring the war home to the American people, especially in the Chesapeake Bay. Warren, who had no stomach for plundering, assigned the command in these waters to Admiral Sir George Cockburn (pronounced Co-burn), a crusty old seadog. Guided through the countryside by runaway slaves, Cockburn devoted the spring of 1813 to plundering the Chesapeake. His immediate aim was to destroy American warships, burn government supplies, and ruin the coastal trade. His larger purpose was to show Americans the futility of resisting British power and the perils of making war on the Mistress of the Seas.

In mid-June Warren returned to the Chesapeake with reinforcements, determined to attack Norfolk, Virginia, a regional commercial center that was harboring the frigate *Constellation.* Warren had to give up the attack, however, because his forces ran into too many natural obstacles as well as heavy artillery fire.

Next the British attacked Hampton, Virginia, with a force of 2,000. The militia units defending the town were brushed aside, and those civilians found in Hampton were subjected to all kinds of abuse. According to Charles Napier, a young British officer who later gained fame in India, "Every horror was committed with impunity: rape, murder, pillage; and not a man was punished!" The British blamed the excesses on the Chasseurs Britannique—French prisoners of war who had enlisted in British service to avoid confinement.

The British depredations caused a great deal of bitterness in the Chesapeake. *Niles' Register* called Warren the "spoiler in the Chesapeake" and dubbed his troops "Water-*Winnebagoes*"—an allusion to the most militant Indians in the Northwest. Cockburn drew even greater fire. "The wantonness of his barbarities," said *Niles,* "have gibbetted him on infamy." Some Americans, however, benefited from the British presence. When they met with no resistance in an area, the British usually paid for the provisions they needed. Those willing to do business with the invaders—and there were many—profited handsomely. In addition, about 600 runaway slaves who found sanctuary with the British were given a choice of either enlisting in the armed services or settling in the West Indies.

❖ ❖ ❖ ❖ ❖

There were fewer naval engagements in 1813 than in 1812 because most American warships were bottled up in port. Even those that managed to escape often returned empty-handed because British warships now sailed in squadrons and British merchantmen in convoys. The Navy Department ordered American warships to cruise separately and to avoid battle except under the most favorable circumstances. There were only four naval duels in this campaign, and three of these ended in defeat for the United States.

In May of 1813 James Lawrence, who had earlier commanded the USS *Hornet* in its victory over the *Peacock,* was given command of the *Chesapeake* (50 guns). The *Chesapeake* was fitted out in Boston, but Lawrence had trouble finding experienced seamen for his crew. Many of the ship's veterans refused to reenlist because of a dispute over prize money, forcing Lawrence to accept raw recruits.

Hovering off the coast of Boston were two British frigates, the *Shannon* (52 guns), commanded by Captain Philip Broke, and the *Tenedos* (38 guns). Broke had been cruising in the *Shannon* since 1806, and unlike other British naval commanders, he drilled his crew in gunnery. According to a British officer who was assigned to the American station, "The *Shannon*'s men were better trained, and understood gunnery better, than any men I ever saw." As the *Chesapeake* was preparing to sail, Broke sent the *Tenedos* away and dispatched a challenge to Lawrence for a meeting "ship to ship, to try the fortunes of our respective flags." Lawrence sailed before this challenge arrived, but he needed no invitation.

On June 1 the *Chesapeake* emerged from port flying a banner that read "Free Trade and Sailor's Rights." Lawrence made for the *Shannon,* but for reasons that are unclear, he passed up a chance to cut across the British ship's stern and rake her. Instead, the two ships lined up parallel to each other and exchanged broadsides at close range. Superior gunnery quickly carried the day for the *Shannon.* The *Chesapeake* lost control, was subjected to a murderous raking fire, and then boarded. Lawrence was mortally wounded but before dying uttered those words that gave him immortality: "Don't give up the ship!" His men, however, suffered heavy casualties and had no choice but to surrender. The British took control of the *Chesapeake* and sailed it into Halifax as a prize of war.

The *Shannon's* victory, which was accomplished in only fifteen minutes, provided a great boost to British morale. It was the first defeat of an American frigate in the war and ended a long string of American naval victories. Broke was made a baronet, given the key to London, and showered with gifts from an appreciative nation.

Lawrence, on the other hand, was given a hero's funeral in New York City that was reportedly attended by 50,000 people. His words—"Don't give up the ship"—became the motto of the young navy and replaced "free trade and sailors' rights" as the rallying cry of the war. The Navy Department paid Lawrence the highest tribute by naming Perry's flagship on Lake Erie after him.

The American frigate *Essex* (46 guns), with Captain David Porter commanding, had better luck, though ultimately it too was captured. Porter was never happy with the *Essex*. It was so overloaded with guns and such a bad sailer that he regarded it as "the worst frigate in the service." Nevertheless, Porter made the most of his cruise in the *Essex*. Rounding the Horn in late 1812, the *Essex* became the first American warship to sail in the Pacific. For over a year Porter cruised in those waters, destroying British whaling ships, taking prizes, and living off the enemy.

In late 1813 the British dispatched a squadron of three ships under the command of Captain James Hillyar to track down and destroy the *Essex*. Two of the British ships, the *Phoebe* (46 guns) and the *Cherub* (26 guns), caught up with the *Essex* at Valparaiso, Chile. Porter sought to persuade Hillyar to fight a duel at sea. Even though the crew of the *Essex* goaded the British with insulting songs, Hillyar refused the challenge. Instead, the two British ships cruised beyond the harbor, waiting for an opportunity to act in concert against the American vessel.

On March 28, 1814, Porter made a run for the sea, but a sudden squall destroyed his topmast, forcing him to seek sanctuary in a small bay. Although the *Essex* was in Chilean waters, the *Phoebe* closed in to take advantage of the ship's distress, and the *Cherub* soon followed. After a hard-fought contest, the *Essex* was forced to strike its colors. Porter bitterly assailed the British officers, not only for refusing a duel but also for attacking the *Essex* while it was in a crippled state in neutral waters.

Two smaller American warships also fought duels with the British. On August 14, 1813, the USS *Argus* (10 guns) was defeated by HMS *Pelican* (11 guns). Another American ship, the *Enterprise* (16 guns), fought HMS *Boxer* (14 guns) on September 5, 1813. The two vessels exchanged broadsides for over an hour before the British ship surrendered. Both captains were killed in the engagement.

With most of the American warships bottled up in port or simply overmatched by the British, privateers in 1813 had to shoulder a heavier burden, though the pickings were slimmer than they had been in 1812. It was difficult to capture British merchantmen on the open seas because most now traveled in convoy. To find prizes, privateers had to cruise in the British West Indies or near the British Isles, for it was only in these waters that merchant ships traveled without an escort.

The most spectacular cruise was made by the *True-Blooded Yankee,* a small vessel fitted out by an American in Paris. On a thirty-seven-day cruise in waters around the British Isles, this ship took twenty-seven prizes, occupied an Irish island for six days, and burned seven vessels in a Scottish harbor. "She outsailed everything," marveled a British naval officer; "not one of our cruisers could touch her." Other privateers also enjoyed successful cruises in 1813, and this kind of warfare continued to bedevil the British, especially in their own waters.

❖ ❖ ❖ ❖ ❖

The outcome of the campaign of 1813 should have occasioned no surprise because the American victories on land and the British victories at sea accorded with the general strengths of the two nations. Although Americans could be justly proud of their triumphs, final victory continued to elude them, and now, more than ever, time was running against them.

In October of 1813 Great Britain's allies had defeated Napoleon in the Battle of Leipzig. Coupled with British triumphs in Spain, this foreshadowed Napoleon's downfall. With these victories behind them, the British began diverting men and materiel to the New World, and this changed the whole complexion of the American war. Having failed to conquer Canada in 1812 or 1813, the United States would not get another chance. When the campaign of 1814 opened, it was the British who were on the offensive.

CHAPTER

4

THE BRITISH COUNTEROFFENSIVE

By the time the campaign of 1814 opened, the initiative in the war had shifted to the British. The Battle of Leipzig the previous October had forced Napoleon to retreat to France, with the Allies in pursuit. On March 31, 1814, the Allies entered Paris. Napoleon abdicated on April 11 and shortly thereafter was exiled to the Mediterranean island of Elba. For the first time in more than a decade, Europe was at peace.

The United States was now alone in the field against England, and most Republicans expected the British to be vindictive. "We should have to fight hereafter," said Joseph Nicholson, "not for 'free trade and sailors' rights,' not for the conquest of the Canadas, but for our national existence." As the character of the war changed, so too did the nation's motto. "Don't give up the soil" gradually replaced "Don't give up the ship."

Since Leipzig, the British had been cautiously detaching veterans from Europe for service in America. After Napoleon's exile, the trickle of troops to the New World turned into a torrent. By September of 1814 some 13,000 veterans had reached Canada, bringing British troop strength there to 30,000. Additional men continued to arrive, so that by the end of the year there were close to 40,000 British troops in the American theater.

Fortunately for the United States, the American army was steadily improving with experience. Two years of campaigning had weeded out many incompetent officers, and Secretary of War John Armstrong, who was a fair judge of talent, had been pushing capable young men ahead. By the spring of 1814 there were about 40,000 men in uniform—a third more than the previous year. Enlistments continued to mount in the remaining months of the war, so that by early 1815 the total was close to 45,000.

❖ ❖ ❖ ❖ ❖

The heaviest fighting on the northern frontier in 1814 took place along the Niagara River. The United States took the offensive on July 3 when Jacob Brown led 3,500 men across the river into Canada. Brown's best troops were those trained by Winfield Scott, who regularly drilled his men seven hours a day.

The American force besieged Fort Erie, compelling the small British garrison there to surrender. From here Brown ordered his army to proceed north in search of the main British force. On July 5, as the Americans approached the Chippewa River, they were harassed by Indians in a nearby forest. Former Congressman Peter B. Porter took charge of a band of militia and Iroquois (roused by the aging Seneca chief Red Jacket) and drove the hostile Indians off. When Porter's troops encountered British regulars, however, they retreated in disorder.

At this point Scott appeared on the scene with a body of regulars that ultimately numbered about 1,500. Soon he had fully engaged a British force of equal size under General Phineas Riall. Despite the hail of artillery fire, Scott's well-disciplined troops, who were dressed in gray rather than blue, maintained their formation and advanced toward the enemy. Riall, who thought the gray uniforms signified militia, was stunned by the tight discipline of the American troops. "Those are regulars, by God!" he reportedly exclaimed, thus contributing to an American legend. Scott's men mounted a bayonet charge that broke the British right flank and forced Riall to retreat across the river. In the Battle of Chippewa, the British suffered 500 killed, wounded, and missing, while American losses were only 325. The American victory was a direct result of the long hours Scott had spent drilling his troops.

Brown next moved his entire army across the Chippewa River, hoping to link up with Chauncey for a combined assault on British bases. Chauncey, however, was ill and, as usual, slow to commit his fleet to action. In addition, he resented Brown's intimation that the navy should carry the army's supplies.

Even without naval support, Brown was determined to seek out the enemy. On July 25 the American army clashed with the British at Lundy's Lane, several miles north of the Chippewa River and not far from Niagara Falls. Scott—always aggressive—attacked a British force of 1,600 to 1,800 with only 1,000 men. Both sides were reinforced, until by dusk the Americans had 2,100 men in the field and the British about 3,000. The confused and bloody battle dragged on well into the night and almost entirely drowned out the roar of Niagara Falls in the background.

Scott's troops pushed back the British left flank and were then reinforced by a detachment under General Eleazar W. Ripley. At the same time, Colonel James Miller's men overran a powerful battery in the center of the British line. British veterans from the Napoleonic Wars claimed they had never seen such a determined attack. "The Americans charged to the very muzzles of our cannon," said one observer, "and actually bayonetted the artillerymen who were at their guns." The British repeatedly counterattacked to regain this battery but were unsuccessful. Brown finally ordered his entire army to withdraw, which brought the battle to an end.

Colonel Miller described the five-hour Battle of Lundy's Lane as "one of the most desperately fought actions ever experienced in America," which was no exaggeration. Brown and Scott were wounded, the latter so seriously that he was knocked out of the war. Both of Britain's senior officers, Riall and Gordon Drummond, were also wounded, and Riall was captured. In all, the United States suffered 850 killed, wounded, or missing in the Battle of Lundy's Lane. Total British losses were about 875. Even though the United States had withdrawn from the field, the losses were about equal, and the battle was a draw.

After Lundy's Lane, the American army—about 2,100 strong and now under the command of General Edmund P. Gaines—retired to Fort Erie. Determined to retake the fort, the British began to pound it with artillery fire on August 13. Then at 2:00 A.M. on August 15, in a heavy rainstorm, three columns of British troops totaling 2,100 men advanced on the fort with fixed bayonets.

Most of the British soldiers had been ordered to remove their flints to ensure surprise. When the attack got under way, the main column stalled, but the other two—led by Colonel Hercules Scott and Lieutenant Colonel William Drummond—penetrated one of the fort's bastions and engaged the defenders in close combat for nearly two hours. Gaines and other Americans heard the British officers calling out to "give the damned Yankee rascals no quarter." The British were finally dislodged when a powder magazine blew up. "The explosion," reported Gaines, "was tremendous—it was decisive." Both commanding British officers were killed. In all, the British suffered 360 killed or wounded and almost 540 captured or missing. Total American losses were only about 130. As the lopsided casualty figures suggest, the Battle of Fort Erie was a great victory for the United States.

Having failed to take Fort Erie by storm, the British mounted three heavy batteries about five hundred yards north of the post, hoping to bombard it into submission. Brown, who had resumed command even though he was still recovering from wounds sustained at Lundy's Lane, rejected advice from his subordinates to evacuate the fort. Instead, he was determined "to storm the [British] batteries, destroy the cannon, and roughly handle the brigade upon duty, before those in reserve could be brought into action."

Two assault forces were formed. One consisted of 1,200 men, mainly New York militia, under Peter Porter; the other was 600 regulars under James Miller. In a driving rainstorm in the middle of the night on September 17, the American troops surprised the British, and after severe fighting overran two of their batteries, spiked the guns, and then retired. The engagement was costly to both sides. The British suffered over 600 casualties, the United States more than 500.

The sortie from Fort Erie was the last in this series of bloody but indecisive engagements on the Niagara front. The American troops evacuated and blew up Fort Erie on November 8 and then retired to the other side of the river.

The battles of Chippewa and Lundy's Lane and the two engagements at Fort Erie contributed to the nation's military tradition by demonstrating that American troops could hold their own against British regulars in close combat. Brown's invasion was nonetheless blunted, and despite the carnage little of strategic importance had been accomplished.

❖ ❖ ❖ ❖ ❖

Although the heaviest fighting took place on the Niagara front, the British concentrated most of their troops farther east. It was here—in upper New York—that they launched their only major offensive on the northern frontier. After building up troop strength in this theater, Sir George Prevost, the governor-general of Canada, devised a plan to march down the western side of Lake Champlain to attack Plattsburgh. He had no intention of holding the town but hoped to occupy some territory to give his government a bargaining chip in the peace negotiations.

Having amassed an army of more than 10,000, Prevost crossed into the United States on August 31, 1814. Secretary of War Armstrong, who did not expect the British to mount a major offensive in this region, had ordered most of the troops out of the area. This left the burden of defense on General Alexander Macomb, who had only 3,400 men at his disposal, many of whom were raw recruits. Although some members of his staff urged Macomb to retreat, he refused. "The eyes of America are on us," he said. "Fortune always favors the brave."

Macomb sent skirmishing parties—consisting mainly of militia—to slow the British march, but these troops were brushed aside. "So undaunted . . . was the enemy," Macomb reported, "that he never deployed in his whole march, always pressing on in column." Prevost halted his men on September 6 on the north side of the Saranac River. Here he waited for support from the British fleet on Lake Champlain.

Both sides had been frantically building ships on the lake, and the two fleets were now about evenly matched. The British squadron was commanded by Captain George Downie and consisted of the *Confiance* (37 guns), *Linnet* (16), *Chub* (11), *Finch* (11), and twelve gunboats mounting a total of 17 guns. The *Confiance*, which had a furnace for hot shot, was the largest ship on the lake—far superior to anything the United States had—but it was not quite ready for action. In fact, the last carpenters did not leave the ship until just before it reached Plattsburgh Bay. Downie was opposed by thirty-year-old Lieutenant Thomas Macdonough, whose fleet consisted of the *Saratoga* (26 guns), *Eagle* (20), *Ticonderoga* (17), *Preble* (7), and ten gunboats carrying 16 guns. Although the British had a decided advantage in long guns, the United States had the edge in short guns, or carronades.

Macdonough anchored his fleet near Cumberland Head in Plattsburgh Bay to await Downie's attack. The American ships were positioned in such a way that the British could not use their long guns to good effect. Instead, they would have to move in close, where Macdonough's guns were likely to be more effective. Macdonough also put out the anchors of his larger ships so that if necessary he could wind the vessels around and bring fresh batteries to bear on the enemy. This, as it turned out, gave him a decisive advantage in the battle that ensued.

At 8:00 A.M. on September 11, Downie rounded Cumberland Head and engaged Macdonough's fleet. Early in the contest each side lost a ship. HMS *Chub* drifted out of control toward the shore, where it surrendered to American troops. The USS *Preble* was also disabled and drifted out of the battle. Both commanding officers were hit during the battle. Downie was killed instantly when struck by a carriage knocked loose from a cannon. His watch was flattened by the blow, marking the exact time of his death. Macdonough was twice knocked down and dazed, first by the head of a decapitated midshipman and then by flying debris.

The *Saratoga* was set on fire by hot shot from the *Confiance,* and eventually its entire battery was silenced by enemy fire. Macdonough, however, was able to wind his ship around by using the anchors he had set before the battle. This enabled him to bring a fresh battery into the contest. Lieutenant James Robertson, who had taken command of the *Confiance* after Downie's death, tried to bring his ship around by employing the same maneuver, but without advance preparation his lines became fouled. The *Confiance* took such a terrific pounding from Macdonough's fresh battery—105 shot-holes were later counted in its hull—that members of the crew refused to continue the fight.

Two and a half hours into the battle, the *Confiance* surrendered. The *Linnet* followed suit. The *Finch,* which had lost control and had run aground off Crab Island, also surrendered. Only the gunboats, which had fled in the heat of battle, escaped. Echoing Perry after his great victory on Lake Erie, Macdonough sent a message to the secretary of the navy that read, "The Almighty has been pleased to grant us a signal victory on Lake Champlain in the capture of one frigate, one brig, and two sloops of war of the enemy."

Meanwhile, Prevost had ordered his men to attack Macomb's position on land. British troops under the command of General Sir Frederick Robinson crossed the Saranac River and routed the militia on the other side. Robinson's men paused to wait for reinforcements, but just then Prevost learned of Downie's defeat on the lake. Fearing that his supply lines would be menaced by the American fleet and the militia pouring into the region, Prevost ordered a retreat. According to Robinson, the British withdrawal was conducted "in the most precipitate and disgraceful manner."

The retreat of such a large force after so little fighting created consternation in both Canada and England. Prevost had already alienated many of his veteran officers by insisting on proper dress, and the retreat only served to increase this antagonism. According to one observer, "The recent disgraceful business of Plattsburgh has so completely irritated the feelings of the whole army that it is in a state almost amounting to mutiny."

Macdonough, on the other hand, was showered with praise and rewards. He received a gold medal from Congress, a thousand acres of land in Cayuga County from the state of New York, and a hundred acres on Cumberland Head from Vermont. Other states and cities gave him valuable keepsakes. "In one month," he said, "from a poor lieutenant I became a rich man."

The battles on Lake Champlain and at Plattsburgh closed out the fighting on the northern frontier in 1814. In spite of growing British strength in Canada, the fighting there continued to be indecisive. After three years of campaigning, the war on the Canadian-American frontier was still a stalemate.

❖ ❖ ❖ ❖ ❖

British operations on the Atlantic Coast were more successful than those on the Canadian frontier because here they could use their fleet to support their troops. The British targeted two areas for amphibious operations in this theater: Maine and the Chesapeake Bay. British officials coveted northern Maine because it jutted into Canada, hampering overland transportation between Quebec and Halifax. The Canadian-American boundary was in dispute here, and by occupying part of Maine, the British hoped to settle the dispute in their favor.

Accordingly, in the summer of 1814 a large British force occupied Eastport, Castine, and other towns on the northern Maine coast. The inhabitants were given a choice of taking an oath to keep the peace or leaving the area. They were also urged to take an oath of allegiance to the British Crown. Those who took this oath were accorded the same commercial privileges British subjects had. Castine became a British port of entry and a resort town for army and naval officers on leave.

Most of the inhabitants welcomed the region's new status because it meant increased trade with New Brunswick and Nova Scotia. "It is scarcely possible to conceive the joy of the inhabitants," said a Massachusetts newspaper. "At the striking of the flag, some huzza'd, and others, men of influence, observed, *'now we shall get rid of the tax gatherers,' 'now the damned Democrats will get it.'*" Eastern Maine, like Mackinac and Fort Niagara, remained in British hands until the war was over.

❖ ❖ ❖ ❖ ❖

Far more demoralizing to Americans than the occupation of Maine was the invasion of the Chesapeake. The bay's extensive shoreline was exposed, and the region's two most important cities—Washington and Baltimore—offered inviting targets. A successful attack on the nation's capital would be a great blow to American pride, while an assault on Baltimore would garner considerable prize money and put an end to the use of that city as a base for privateering.

The British established a base on Tangier Island in the Chesapeake and then dispatched a naval force under Captain Robert Barrie to destroy a squadron of gunboats under the command of Joshua Barney. Barrie twice engaged Barney in a tributary of the Patuxent but was driven off by artillery fire from the shore. This enabled Barney to get his boats back into the Patuxent's main branch, though they remained bottled up and later had to be destroyed to prevent them from falling into enemy hands.

These operations were conducted perilously close to the nation's capital, but little was done to prepare Washington for defense. Armstrong was convinced that the capital would never be attacked because it had no strategic importance, and other officials were slow to perceive the danger too. Not until July 1 did President Madison authorize the creation of a special military district embracing the nation's capital. Madison put General William Winder in charge of the new district. Winder had only 500 regulars at his disposal, and the militia units called into service were slow to respond. Winder's inexperience told early, and he seemed overwhelmed by the task before him. He spent much of his time traveling through the countryside inspecting the terrain, while the real work of planning strategy and preparing defensive works remained undone.

By mid-August Admiral Alexander Cochrane and General Robert Ross had arrived in the Chesapeake with twenty warships and several transports filled with veterans from Europe. Also present was Admiral George Cockburn, who knew the area because he had overseen the predatory raids the previous year. After sailing up the Patuxent River, the British landed 4,500 men at Benedict, Maryland, on August 19–20. On August 22 the troops reached Upper Marlboro, where they were joined by Cockburn. Leaving 500 marines at Upper Marlboro, Ross marched his troops toward Bladensburg, where he could cross the eastern branch of the Potomac and approach Washington from the northeast.

By this time American officials realized the capital's peril and began frantically putting the city in a state of defense. Additional militia units were called out, but there was scarcely enough time to prepare them for battle. Most of the men were short of sleep and hungry. The militia-men were joined by some regulars and about 500 sailors and marines under Barney's command.

The American force—perhaps 7,000 troops in all—was arrayed in three lines facing the eastern branch of the Potomac River. The third line was too far away to support the first two, and Secretary of State James Monroe (who had no authority in the matter) redeployed the troops so that the second line could not support the first. The president and other civilian officials arrived on the scene just before the battle began and were on the verge of crossing the bridge into the approaching British columns when they were warned off by a volunteer scout.

About 1:00 P.M. on August 24, just as the last militiamen took their places, the British appeared on the opposite side of the river. The defenders had neglected to destroy the bridge (though the water was shallow enough to ford anyway), and first one British brigade and then another got across the river. The British outflanked the first American line, forcing it to fall back.

Just as the British were attacking the second line, Winder—who had radiated defeat and confusion from the outset—ordered it to fall back. The withdrawal turned into a rout—immortalized in song and verse as "the Bladensburg races." The British use of small Congreve rockets, which did little actual damage but terrified even hardened veterans, contributed to the panic, and doubtless the hundred-degree temperatures added to everyone's discomfort.

Only Barney's troops, which anchored the third line, held firm, tearing into the advancing British units with grapeshot from their heavy naval guns. The British routed the militia protecting Barney's flank and then stormed his position. By this time Barney had run out of ammunition. Although Barney was wounded and captured, most of his men got away. By 4:00 in the afternoon, the British controlled the battlefield. The United States suffered only 70 casualties in the Battle of Bladensburg, while the British sustained 250. The disparity in these figures suggests that with more disciplined troops the United States might have prevailed.

By the time the battle was over, most people—soldiers, officials, and residents alike—had fled from Washington. Dolley Madison oversaw the removal of cabinet records and White House treasures but had to leave her personal property. Most of the other government records were saved, though House clerks were thwarted by the lack of transportation.

Secretary of the Treasury George Campbell had given the president a pair of dueling pistols, but Madison had no occasion to use them. He left them in the White House, from which they were stolen by local marauders. Madison departed with Attorney General Richard Rush for Virginia. On the way they were joined by Monroe and were reportedly subjected to various insults for mismanaging the war.

The British marched into Washington about 8:00 P.M.. Ross looked in vain for someone to parlay with to establish the terms of surrender. A group of British officers headed by Cockburn entered the White House. "We found a supper all ready," one recalled, "which many of us speedily consumed . . . and drank some very good wine also." Having satisfied their appetites, the British took some souvenirs and then set fire to the building. They also burned the Capitol (which included the Library of Congress), the Treasury, and the building housing the War and State departments.

Although most private buildings were spared, Cockburn personally supervised the destruction of the office of the semiofficial *National Intelligencer,* amusing spectators "with much of the peculiar slang of the common sewer in relation to the editors." The paper's owners took this surprisingly well. When the *Intelligencer* resumed publication, it carried an editorial praising the British for their restraint. "Greater respect was certainly paid to private property than has usually been exhibited by the enemy in his marauding parties. No houses were half as much *plundered* by the enemy as by the knavish wretches about the town who profited of the general distress."

The fires set by the British burned all night. A pair of storms followed the next day, one of which was so violent that it blew down several buildings, killing some British soldiers inside. Others perished when a dry well containing powder exploded. "The effect was terrific," said the *National Intelligencer.* "Every one of [the] soldiers near was blown into eternity, many at a greater distance wounded, and the excavation remains an evidence of the great force of this explosion." The British departed from the city on August 25, reembarking at Benedict on August 30.

Meanwhile, Madison and his cabinet had returned to Washington on August 27. Some people blamed the destruction of the capital on the president, and rumors were afloat that his life was in danger. Graffiti appeared on the walls of the Capitol that read: "George Washington founded this city after a seven years' war with England—James Madison lost it after a two years' war." Most people in the capital, however, blamed Armstrong, a northerner who many thought had intentionally sacrificed the city. Local militia refused to take orders from Armstrong, and after meeting with the president, he retired to Baltimore and subsequently submitted his resignation. Madison named Monroe acting secretary of war.

Most people in England rejoiced at the embarrassment of their enemy and considered the destruction of Washington just retaliation for American depredations in Canada. The prince regent called the Chesapeake campaign "brilliant and successful," and Ross was officially commended. The park and tower guns in London were fired at noon three days in succession to celebrate the victory, and the *Times* and *Courier* were reportedly "nettled that [British] commanders did not date their dispatches from the Capital."

❖ ❖ ❖ ❖ ❖

In early September the British decided to follow up on their success at Washington by attacking Baltimore. This city was an attractive target not only because it was a large commercial center and an important base for privateers but also because it was such a hotbed of Anglophobia. Since early 1813 Samuel Smith, a United States senator and major general in the militia, had been working with other volunteers to prepare the city for defense. By the middle of 1814 Smith had gathered 10,000 to 15,000 troops (mostly militia) and had every available man building earthworks.

Ross landed his army—about 4,500 men—at North Point at 3:00 A.M. on September 12. Five hours later the troops began their march to Baltimore fourteen miles away. About halfway to the city they met a force of 3,200 militia under the command of General John Stricker. The British softened the American lines with artillery and then launched a frontal assault that forced the Americans to retreat. The Americans lost 215 men, the British 340. Although the Battle of North Point was a British victory, it was a costly one, for Ross was killed by a sniper. "It is impossible to conceive the effect which this melancholy spectacle produced throughout the army," recalled a British officer. Ross's body was shipped to England in a cask of rum for burial, and thereafter the British gave no quarter to snipers.

Colonel Arthur Brooke assumed command after Ross's death and resumed the march to Baltimore. On September 13 the British came within sight of the city's defenses. Here they waited for the British navy to pound the Americans into submission.

By this time, Cochrane had brought up his bomb and rocket ships to attack Fort McHenry, which was defended by 1,000 men under the command of Major George Armistead. Cochrane hoped to silence the guns of the fort so he could bring his lighter ships into Baltimore Harbor to bombard the American lines. The British fired more than 1,500 rounds at the fort over a twenty-five-hour period on September 13–14. About 400 of these rounds found their mark, but the damage was minimal. Only 4 Americans were killed and 24 wounded.

Francis Scott Key, a Georgetown Federalist who had come to Baltimore with a volunteer artillery company, had boarded a British ship to secure the release of a prisoner. Although he achieved his mission, the British kept him on board until after the attack on Fort McHenry was over. Key paced the ship all night witnessing the bombardment. On the morning of September 14, after seeing the fort's huge flag still flying, Key was inspired to write "The Star-Spangled Banner," which he put to an eighteenth-century British drinking song, "To Anacreon in Heaven." ("The bombs bursting in air" were the British mortar shells that exploded above the fort; "the rockets' red glare" refers to Congreve rockets.) Key's song became an instant hit, but not until 1931 did Congress make it the national anthem.

The failure of the attack on Fort McHenry doomed the British campaign against Baltimore. Unable to secure naval support or to lure the Americans out from behind their defensive works, General Brooke decided to call off the attack. At 3:00 A.M. on September 14, with campfires still burning, the British army left for the coast, where it reembarked on transports.

The Battle of Baltimore ended the Chesapeake campaign. Local reports indicated that during the campaign British troops had looted private property, destroyed church property, and even opened coffins in their search for booty. "Their conduct," said Congressman Robert Wright, "would have disgraced cannibals."

The British were also accused of fomenting a slave rebellion. Although this was untrue, Cochrane did issue a proclamation that promised all interested Americans a "choice of either entering into His Majesty's sea or land forces, or of being sent as FREE settlers to the British possessions in North America or the West Indies." Some 300 runaway slaves took advantage of this offer and entered British service.

According to Cochrane, they showed "extraordinary steadiness and good conduct when in action with the enemy." When the British departed, they carried off more than 2,000 runaways, most of whom settled in Canada.

❖ ❖ ❖ ❖ ❖

Although the British did not realize it at the time, the Chesapeake campaign was the high-water mark of their counteroffensive in 1814. Their next campaign—against the Gulf Coast—ended in disaster. Initially, they saw this campaign as a means of taking the pressure off Canada. By the time the operation got under way, however, they were primarily interested in occupying territory that might be used in bargaining at the peace negotiations.

The Gulf Coast attracted the British because it was sparsely populated and lightly defended. New Orleans, located a hundred miles up the Mississippi River, was a particularly tempting target. With a population of almost 25,000, it was the largest city west of the Appalachian Mountains. It was also the principal outlet for western commodities, and millions of dollars in produce were blockaded in the port. Scottish naval officers like Cochrane were known to have a keen eye for booty, and the British brought cargo ships with them to carry off their plunder. Indeed, British prisoners of war and deserters later claimed that the watchword and countersign on the morning of the Battle of New Orleans was "beauty and booty."

To secure access to the interior, the British in August of 1814 occupied the forts at Pensacola, a Spanish port city that had the best harbor on the Gulf Coast. The following month they launched an unsuccessful attack against Mobile, a port city in West Florida that the United States had seized from Spain in 1813.

On November 7, 1814, Andrew Jackson responded to the British threat by attacking Pensacola with a force of 4,100 regulars, militia, and Indians. The Spanish governor, who had perhaps 500 troops at his disposal, could not decide whether to surrender or to defend the city, and Jackson marched in almost unopposed. Disgusted, the British blew up the forts they occupied and retired to the Apalachicola River. With its forts destroyed, Pensacola was neutralized, and Jackson abandoned the city and marched to Mobile. Almost belatedly—since he fully expected the British to attack Mobile first—he raced to New Orleans, arriving in the Crescent City on December 1.

Jackson's arrival in New Orleans had a dramatic effect on the people. "General Jackson," wrote one contemporary, "electrified all hearts." After making a detailed study of the area, Jackson ordered all the water approaches from the Gulf blocked and batteries established at strategic points. He also established an excellent intelligence system to keep abreast of enemy movements.

Governor William Claiborne called out all the militia in the area, and troops began to pour in from miles around. John Coffee force-marched 850 Tennessee riflemen from Baton Rouge, reportedly covering 135 miles in three days. Jackson already had appealed to free black men to enlist in the regular army, and he now accepted the services of a special corps of black troops, mostly refugees from Santo Domingo, raised by Colonel Jean Baptiste Savary.

The Baratarian pirates also offered their services. The pirates had long infested the Gulf Coast waters, preying on commerce and smuggling their booty into New Orleans. Although Jackson had earlier described them as "hellish banditti," he could use more men and desperately needed the artillery and ammunition the pirates had. He therefore reluctantly accepted their offer. The Baratarians not only augmented Jackson's force but proved to be excellent artillerymen. Their knowledge of the local terrain was also invaluable. Jean Laffite (or Lafitte), the Baratarian leader, got along so well with Jackson that he became the general's unofficial aide-de-camp.

Meanwhile, the British had been assembling a large army in Jamaica—about 10,000 strong—for their Gulf Coast campaign. The command was assigned to General Edward Pakenham, an able and experienced officer who was the Duke of Wellington's brother-in-law. At the end of November most of the British troops were put on board transports in a large convoy—commanded by Cochrane—and shipped to the Gulf Coast.

Because they lacked the necessary small boats to operate farther north, the British decided to attack through Lake Borgne. As they moved toward the lake, they found their way blocked by Lieutenant Thomas ap Catesby Jones, who had five gunboats and 185 men. Jones had been sent to keep an eye out for the British, not to do battle with them. But he lost his wind, and since his boats were not equipped with oars, he had little choice but to prepare for battle. To destroy the American force, the British sent an assault force of forty-five boats and 1,200 men under the command of Captain Nicholas Lockyer. In the engagement that followed on December 14, the British prevailed but suffered about 100 casualties. Jones lost about 40 killed and wounded. The rest of his men were captured.

Having disposed of Jones's force, the British established a base on Pea Island. The weather was cold and windy, and although primitive shanties were erected for the officers, everyone suffered. "Neither day nor night," a British naval officer complained, "can we contrive to make ourselves comfortably warm." After hiring some Spanish and Portuguese fishermen as guides, the British advanced across Lake Borgne and several bayous to Jacques Villeré's plantation, which was located on the Mississippi River eight miles below New Orleans. Here they established their headquarters for the campaign.

Jackson was determined to meet the British well beyond New Orleans and to fight them before they were at full strength. As soon as he learned of their arrival at Villeré's, he rounded up 1,800 men and marched them to within a mile of the British position. Jackson's men were supported by two ships, the *Carolina* (14 guns) and the *Louisiana* (22 guns).

At 7:30 at night on December 23, the *Carolina* opened fire on the British camp, and shortly thereafter Jackson ordered his army to attack. The British troops, who were under the command of General John Keane, were unaware of Jackson's presence and were caught by surprise. Much close fighting ensued, resulting in a large number of bayonet wounds. The lines were not clearly drawn, and in the darkness, smoke, and fog there was considerable confusion on both sides. Friendly troops fired on each other or blundered into enemy lines. By the time the battle ended, the British had suffered 275 casualties, the Americans 215.

British reinforcements began to arrive the following day, and the day after that (Christmas Day) Pakenham himself arrived with additional troops, bringing the total British strength to more than 4,000 men. In the days that followed, the Americans constructed earthworks along a canal between a cypress swamp on the east and the Mississippi River on the west. At the same time, the American ships in the river continued to bombard British positions, while Tennessee and Choctow sharpshooters harassed British pickets. The British found the sniper fire particularly infuriating. "To us," said an officer, "it appeared an ungenerous return to barbarity."

The British managed to blow up the *Carolina* with hot shot on December 27. The next day Pakenham ordered his troops to advance in two columns toward the American lines, which were now defended by about 4,000 men. The British suffered such intense fire, not only from the American troops but also from the *Louisiana* (which fired 800 rounds), that Pakenham gave up the attack and ordered a withdrawal. In this engagement, the losses on both sides were light: perhaps 35 for the United States and 55 for the British.

Jackson used the respite to good advantage to strengthen his position. He extended his defensive works farther into the swamp, so that his line was now a mile long. He also established additional artillery batteries in his line, bringing the total to eight. As a hedge against disaster, he built two additional lines closer to the city in case his men had to fall back. In addition, he ordered the construction of a defensive line on the western side of the river to be anchored by naval guns taken from the *Louisiana*.

After getting the worse of an artillery duel on December 31, Pakenham waited for reinforcements that were en route to his camp. Each soldier brought a cannon ball in his knapsack to replenish the supply in the front lines. When a boat loaded with these troops overturned on Lake Borgne, the extra weight carried many of the soldiers to the bottom. Those troops who made it safely to Pakenham's camp raised his total strength to about 6,000 men.

Meanwhile, Cochrane had taken advantage of the lull in the fighting to dam Villeré Canal. He hoped to bring boats through the canal to ferry 1,500 troops across the Mississippi River. The number of boats actually brought forward, however, made it possible to move only 600 troops to the opposite shore.

The British battle plan called for Colonel William Thornton to lead the 600 troops across the river and launch a night attack against the American position there, which was defended by 700 ill-trained Louisiana and Kentucky militia under the command of General David Morgan. Thornton was to seize the American guns and turn them on Jackson's main line across the river. Then at dawn Pakenham's principal force, about 5,300 strong, was to advance in three columns across Chalmette's plantation to Jackson's main line, which was now defended by 4,700 men.

Thornton fell behind schedule and did not launch his attack until nearly daylight on January 8. His troops completely routed the militia but had no chance to follow up on their victory. The British attack on the other side of the river had stalled, and Thornton's men were ordered to withdraw.

The main British force attacked about an hour and a half after Thornton. A fog covered the advance for a time, but it lifted suddenly, leaving the British troops completely exposed to American fire. When the British got within 500 yards, the Americans began firing their cannons; when they were within 300 yards, American riflemen opened up; and when they got within 100 yards, those with muskets opened fire. The effect of this fire—particularly the grape and canister from the American cannons—was utterly devastating. According to a British veteran of the Napoleonic Wars, it was "the most murderous [fire] I ever beheld before or since."

All along the battle line the British were mowed down before they could get near the American earthworks. Only a small column advancing along the river got to the American line, but these troops suffered such a withering fire that they had to fall back. The fire was so intense that many hardened British veterans turned and fled. Others hit the ground and remained there until the battle was over. Pakenham did his best to rally his men, but as he rode across the battlefield he made a conspicuous target. One horse was shot out from under him, and shortly after commandeering another, he was "cut asunder by a cannon ball."

General John Lambert, who took command after Pakenham fell, broke off the engagement. It had lasted only a half-hour on the eastern side of the river, and yet the carnage was terrific. One eyewitness said the field was a terrible sight to behold, "with dead and wounded laying in heaps"—all wearing scarlet British uniforms. Those British soldiers who had thrown themselves to the ground in the heat of battle got up when the fighting ended. A few fled, but most surrendered. One officer who was far from American lines reportedly surrendered because "*these damned Yankee riflemen can pick a squirrel's eye out as far as they can see it.*"

The battle on January 8, 1815—which was *the* Battle of New Orleans—was the most lopsided engagement of the war. The British lost over 2,000 men (including close to 500 captured). The United States, by contrast, lost only about 70 men, and only 13 on Jackson's side of the river.

Jackson realized that the British attack was over but was reluctant to loosen his grip on New Orleans. On December 16 he had proclaimed martial law, mainly to prevent spies from moving freely into and out of the city. Although reports of peace arrived as early as February 19, 1815, he refused to lift martial law until official news came on March 13.

In the meantime, he continued his dictatorial rule in the city. When a member of the legislature wrote a newspaper article complaining, Jackson had him jailed, and when a federal judge ordered the victim released, Jackson imprisoned the judge. When the war ended, the judge fined Jackson $1,000 for contempt of court. "The only question," he said, "was whether the law should bend to the general or the general to the law." (In 1844 Congress refunded Jackson's fine, with interest— $2,732 in all.)

Jackson also dealt severely with 200 Tennessee militiamen who had allegedly deserted in September of 1814. Although ordered out for six months' duty, the men were convinced that they could be required to serve only three months and hence had gone home. Jackson ordered the men seized and tried by military tribunal in Mobile in December of 1814. The court found the men guilty. Most were sentenced to forfeit part of their pay and make up lost time and then were drummed out of camp with their heads partly shaved. The six ringleaders—a sergeant and five privates—did not get off so easily. Convicted of desertion and mutiny, they were executed by a firing squad on February 21, 1815. Although the Battle of New Orleans catapulted Jackson into the limelight, his enemies never let the public forget his severe brand of military justice.

❖ ❖ ❖ ❖ ❖

The United States made a good showing in the fighting on land in the campaign of 1814. On the northern frontier, American troops had defeated the British at Chippewa, fought them to a draw at Lundy's Lane, and beat them twice at Fort Erie. American forces also had compelled the British to retreat from Plattsburgh—a result of Macdonough's great victory on Lake Champlain. On the Atlantic Coast the British had occupied eastern Maine and burned the nation's capital, but they had been repulsed at Baltimore. Moreover, they had suffered one of the greatest military disasters in British history when they attacked New Orleans.

The American victories were largely a tribute to good leadership— Scott, Brown, Macomb, and Macdonough in the North; Smith at Baltimore; and Jackson at New Orleans. After two years of campaigning, Madison finally had found competent generals to fight his war.

❖ ❖ ❖ ❖ ❖

The war at sea continued to favor the British in 1814. The most effective use of British sea power was still their blockade. The Royal Navy had blockaded the middle and southern states in 1812–13, and in April of 1814 the blockade was extended to New England. The British decided to close New England's ports to put an end to neutral trade and to prevent warships there from getting to sea.

The extension of the British blockade further curtailed American trade and reduced government revenue. American exports, which had reached $61.3 million in 1811, steadily plunged during the war to a low of $6.9 million in 1814. There was a similar decline in imports, from $53.4 million in 1811 to $13.0 million in 1814. Even though Congress had doubled the customs duties at the beginning of the war, revenue from this source fell from $13.3 million in 1811 to $6.0 million in 1814.

The economic bottlenecks that had appeared in 1813 worsened in 1814 as the gluts and shortages in every market increased. Merchants and fishermen could not send their ships to sea, and farmers could not get their produce to foreign markets. The shipping industry was particularly hard hit. The tonnage of American ships engaged in foreign trade dropped from 948,000 in 1811 to 60,000 in 1814. Although some of these losses were offset by new economic activities—such as privateering and manufacturing—the overall effect of the war on the American economy was decidedly negative.

Great Britain's naval presence was felt in other ways. The number of predatory raids increased in 1814, particularly along the lengthy and exposed New England coast, which heretofore had been untouched. In one raid a British squadron sailed up the Connecticut River and destroyed twenty-seven vessels valued at $140,000. The militia was repeatedly called out to guard against raids like this, and life in many cities—large and small like—was thoroughly disrupted.

The Royal Navy also cut off the nation's coastal islands from the mainland. Although Nantucket was dominated by Republicans who supported the war, by August of 1814 the threat of starvation was so acute that the island had to declare its neutrality. In exchange for surrendering its public stores, supplying British warships, and discontinuing the payment of federal taxes, Nantucket won the right to import provisions and fuel from the mainland and to fish in nearby waters.

Other exposed towns also came to terms with the British. On Cape

Cod many paid tribute to avoid bombardment and plundering. On Block Island (which was part of Rhode Island) people were "in the daily habit of carrying intelligence and succor to the enemy's squadron," which prompted American officials to cut off all trade with the island. British officers were shocked by the eagerness with which Americans pursued their own interest at the expense of the nation's. "Self, the great ruling principle," said one, "[is] more powerful with Yankees than any people I ever saw."

❖   ❖   ❖   ❖   ❖

Most American warships were bottled up in port in 1814, and the navy actually suffered its greatest losses to British troops operating inland. The occupation of Washington forced Americans to destroy the *Columbia* (rated at 44 guns) and the *Argus* (rated at 22), and the seizure of eastern Maine forced them to burn the *Adams* (28 guns).

The nation's greatest loss at sea in this campaign was the *President*, a heavy frigate mounting 52 guns. This vessel had such a fine reputation that in 1812 Captain William Bainbridge, who commanded the *Constitution*, had offered John Rodgers $5,000 to trade ships. Rodgers had refused, which enabled Bainbridge to make his reputation in the *Constitution*.

By 1815 Captain Stephen Decatur commanded the *President*. Taking advantage of a severe snowstorm, he sailed out of New York Harbor. Though considered a good sailer, the ship ran aground on a sandbar and got so twisted around before breaking free that it lost much of its speed. The *President* was subsequently chased by a squadron of British ships that included three light frigates, the *Endymion* (40 guns), *Pomone* (38), and *Tenedos* (38). In an engagement that took place on January 15, Decatur managed to disable the *Endymion*, but he lost a fifth of his crew, and his ship was crippled, so he surrendered to the other frigates.

The *Constitution* (52 guns), on the other hand, continued its run of good luck. Commanded now by Captain Charles Stewart, the *Constitution* slipped out of Boston Harbor in December of 1814. On February 20, 1815, two hundred miles from Madeira, it met two British ships, the *Cyane* (34), under Captain Gordon Falcon, and the *Levant* (20), under Captain George Douglass. The British commanders were so confident of their seamanship that instead of fleeing they engaged the *Constitution*. The American ship was superbly handled by Stewart and his men, and their gunnery was equally sharp. The *Constitution* was able to rake both its antagonists without being raked itself, and as a result both British ships were forced to surrender. The *Constitution* had to abandon its prizes when chased by a British squadron, but "Old Ironsides" made it back to port with its reputation much enhanced.

The United States constructed six new sloops during the war. Like the heavy frigates, they were designed to outsail any ship they could not outfight. Although finding guns and crews for these vessels was difficult, three of them—the *Hornet* (20 guns), *Peacock* (22), and *Wasp* (22)—made successful cruises in 1814. These vessels captured a number of British ships, including the *Penguin* (19), *Reindeer* (19), *Avon* (18), and *Epervier* (18). The British, in turn, captured the *Frolic* (22), *Syren* (16), and *Rattlesnake* (16). The *Wasp* was lost at sea when it went down with all hands, doubtless during a storm.

The United States launched two ships-of-the-line in 1814, the *Independence* in June and the *Washington* in October. Apart from a small battleship built and given to France during the Revolution, these were the first such vessels constructed in the United States. Both were poorly designed, and neither was ready for sea before the end of the war.

Robert Fulton launched the world's first steam frigate, *Fulton the First*, in October of 1814. This vessel was built for the protection of New York Harbor, but the war ended before it could be given a fair test. Fulton and others also experimented with submarines and mines (which contemporaries called "torpedoes"). Several attempts were made to use crude submarines to attach mines to blockading British ships but without success.

American warships and privateers continued to harass British commerce in the last year of the war. According to the *Naval Chronicle*, "The depredations committed on our commerce by American ships of war and privateers has attained an extent beyond all former precedent." Insurance rates for British vessels sailing from Liverpool to Halifax jumped to 30 percent of the value of the ship and cargo, and underwriters publicly complained about their losses. "Each daily book at Lloyd's [the principal insurer of merchant vessels]," said one, "presents a *tremendous* list for our contemplation."

The favorite haunt for American privateers in 1814 was the British Isles. British merchantmen trading in these waters were not required to sail in convoy and thus made easy targets for privateers, which "in summer weather and light breezes eluded all attempts of the king's ships to catch them." American privateers were particularly active in the Irish

Sea, and insurance rates for ships trading between England and Ireland rose to an unprecedented 13 percent. According to the *Naval Chronicle*, this rate was *"three times higher* than it was when we were at war with all Europe!"

A number of privateers recorded spectacular cruises in 1814. The *Prince-de-Neufchatel* captured or destroyed $1 million in British property in a single cruise. The *Governor Tompkins* stripped and burned fourteen prizes in the English Channel, while the *Harpy* returned to the United States after a twenty-day cruise with booty worth more than $400,000. Captain Thomas Boyle, who commanded the *Chasseur*—"the pride of Baltimore"—added insult to injury by sailing into a British port and issuing a proclamation that mocked British blockade notices. Boyle announced a blockade of "all the ports, harbors, bays, creeks, rivers, inlets, outlets, islands, and sea coast of the United Kingdom of G. Britain and Ireland."

Even when privateers were cornered by British warships, they sometimes offered stout resistance. In September of 1814 British boarding parties from nearby warships attacked the *General Armstrong* while it lay in a neutral port in the Azores. Ultimately the privateer was abandoned by its crew, but the British had suffered close to 200 casualties compared with only 9 for the United States. British officials were so embarrassed by their losses that they refused to allow any mail on the vessels that carried their wounded back to England.

The following month HMS *Endymion* (40 guns) found itself becalmed off Nantucket in sight of the privateer *Prince-de-Neufchatel* (17). The American ship had just completed a successful cruise and had more than $200,000 in prize goods on board. It had manned so many prizes that its original crew had shrunk from 150 to 40. The captain of the British frigate sent his boats to take the vessel, but the attack failed. The British lost 100 men, while the Americans lost only 30. The privateer had only ten healthy seaman at the end of the engagement, but it managed to escape and reached port safely.

❖   ❖   ❖   ❖   ❖

All in all, the campaign of 1814 turned out well for the United States. Although thrown on the defensive, the nation was able to defeat British offensives everywhere except in Maine and Washington. In all three campaigns during the war (1812, 1813, and 1814), the defending side had fared better than the attacking side, perhaps because most offensive operations required moving men and materiel long distances over rough and heavily wooded terrain. After three years of campaigning, neither the United States nor Great Britain could claim any great advantage in the war, let alone victory. Militarily, the War of 1812 ended in a draw.

5

THE INNER WAR

The War of 1812 was fought not only against the British on the frontiers and the high seas but also among Americans at home. There was bickering, backbiting, and disloyalty in the cabinet. In addition, the administration feuded with Congress, Republicans in Congress feuded with one another, and Republicans everywhere feuded with Federalists. This "inner war" had a direct impact on the prosecution of the real war.

The internal fighting was partly a result of honest differences of opinion. Was the war just, necessary, and winable, or was it an ill-advised invitation to disaster? Should the war be prosecuted in Canada (where Britain was most vulnerable) or on the high seas (where most of the encroachments on American rights had occurred)? Should the nation raise long-term regulars, or should it rely on short-term volunteers and militia? Should it construct ships-of-the-line and frigates (to fight Britain's fleet) or sloops, schooners, and privateers (to cruise against British commerce)? These were questions over which honest people could differ.

Politics also played a part in the inner war. Hoping to lay claim to the nation's successes and avoid blame for its defeats, individuals and factions courted the voters and jockeyed for position. Despite the nation's peril, political considerations were never far from the surface in this war.

The differences in the president's cabinet were both personal and political. Monroe was jealous of any potential rival for the presidency, and Armstrong alienated everyone with his arrogance and indolence. Moreover, Postmaster General Gideon Granger filled positions at his disposal with people openly hostile to the administration. In short, Madison was not master of his own house.

The Republicans in Congress were also deeply divided. The War Hawks and other regular Republicans often differed on policy matters, and the opposition of dissident groups—the Old Republicans, Clintonians, and Senate "Invisibles"—was sometimes implacable. According to one administration supporter, "The malcontent junto of self-called Republicans was worse" than the Federalists.

❖ ❖ ❖ ❖ ❖

Factionalism played a significant role in the election of 1812 and very nearly cost Madison his office. Although voters usually rally around a wartime president, Madison fared worse in 1812 than he had in 1808. Many people—including a sizable number of Republicans—wondered whether "Little Jemmy" (who was only five feet four inches tall) was big enough for the job.

Although a congressional caucus renominated Madison in the spring of 1812, Republicans from New York and other northern states endorsed De Witt Clinton. So too did the Federalists. Clinton's followers saw him as a bold and energetic leader who was friendly to commerce and the navy. In pro-war states, he was portrayed as a man who would shorten the war by prosecuting it more vigorously; in anti-war states, he was presented as a man who would achieve this end by negotiating with the British.

The means of selecting presidential electors varied from state to state. Half chose their electors by popular vote, while the rest left the choice to the legislature. Each state followed its own timetable, and the results drifted in over a two-month period in the fall of 1812. The voting followed the same sectional pattern that the vote on the declaration of war had. Clinton fared best in the North, Madison in the South and West. The key was Pennsylvania, which enjoyed a booming wartime prosperity and cast its 25 electoral votes for Madison. In all, Madison won 128 electoral votes to Clinton's 89. In 1808, by contrast, Madison had defeated his Federalist opponent by a margin of 122 votes to 47.

The Republicans also lost ground in the congressional elections of 1812. The proportion of seats they held fell from 75 to 63 percent in the House and from 82 to 78 percent in the Senate. Nor did they fare much better in the elections of 1814. Although their strength in the House rose slightly, to 65 percent, their strength in the Senate slid to 67 percent. The Republicans suffered even greater losses in state elections. In 1811 they controlled fourteen of seventeen states. By 1813 they controlled only eleven of eighteen. The Federalists made steady gains and by 1813 controlled all five New England states.

Although the Republicans remained in charge of the national government and most of the states throughout the war, the election results indicated that many people questioned not only the administration's handling of the war but also the wisdom of the war itself. The Federalists profited from this discontent, registering their most impressive gains since the 1790s.

❖ ❖ ❖ ❖ ❖

The administration had trouble raising the troops it needed to fight the war. Congress gradually increased the authorized level of the regular army from 10,000 to 62,500, but filling the ranks was difficult. "Money usually can command men," said one Federalist, "but it will take millions to make soldiers of the happy people of this country—nothing short of a little fortune will induce our farmers or their sons to enter a life which they cordially despise: that of a common soldier." This was no exaggeration. To spur enlistments, Congress gradually raised the bounty from $12 in 1811 to $124 and 320 acres of land in 1814. This was a princely sum—more than most unskilled laborers (who earned only $10 or $12 a month) made in two years—probably the equivalent of $25,000 today.

In spite of these incentives, the ranks of the army were never full, and recruitment lagged behind need. Frustrated in its attempts to raise men by conventional means, the administration in 1814 recommended conscripting militia into the army. This elicited a ferocious outcry from Federalist New England. No less a figure than Daniel Webster, who was at the dawn of a long and distinguished public career, urged the New England states to nullify the law—"to interpose between their citizens and arbitrary power." Facing this resistance, Congress backed away from the proposal, and the administration had to be content with voluntary enlistments.

There was also disagreement over the navy. Initially most Republicans opposed naval expansion, believing that a fleet was too costly and would be overwhelmed by the British in the first days of the war. With the spectacular naval victories in 1812, however, many Republicans had a change of heart. In the flush of excitement, Congress authorized four ships-of-the-line, six heavy frigates, and six sloops. Twenty schooners were later added. Although few of these vessels were completed before the war's end, this legislation committed the nation to a long-term construction program.

In the absence of a sizable fleet, the nation had to rely on privateers to carry on the war at sea. To stimulate privateering, Congress lowered the duties on prize goods and offered bounties for the destruction of enemy vessels and the capture of enemy naval personnel. Whether this legislation actually stimulated privateering is unclear, but there is no denying that American privateers menaced British trade in all corners of the globe throughout the war.

Congress was less amenable to building coastal fortifications. Although most of the nation's cities were exposed to attack via the sea, a comprehensive system of fortifications would require massive expenditures and years of labor, and some Republicans preferred to abandon the cities altogether. In the end Congress appropriated only $1 million for this purpose. As a result, coastal cities had to rely heavily on the militia to fend off invasion, an expedient that was both costly and disruptive.

❖　❖　❖　❖　❖

The issue of wartime finance was even more divisive. Prior to the war Secretary of the Treasury Albert Gallatin devised a plan that called for using tax revenue to finance the government's regular expenses and loans to finance the costs of the war. In a report submitted to Congress in January of 1812, Gallatin presented the details, which included doubling the customs duties and reimposing the excise taxes that had contributed to the Federalist defeat in 1800.

Gallatin's report—particularly the proposed excise taxes—created an uproar among Republicans, many of whom feared that the new taxes would render their party and the war unpopular. One Republican accused Gallatin of trying "to chill the war spirit," and a Republican newspaper insisted that his aim was to "*frighten the War Hawks*" and "*blow up the cabinet.*" Although Congress ultimately endorsed the report, it specified that no new taxes would be levied until after war had been declared. Moreover, some Republicans continued to assure their constituents that the war could be won without additional taxes.

Shortly after the declaration of war Republicans voted to double the customs duties, but they refused to impose the excise taxes that they had endorsed only a few months before. "It was admitted by the ruling party in debate," said a Virginia Federalist, "that to impose them now would endanger their success at the next election."

Federalists vigorously protested, claiming that Republican tax poli-cy discriminated against the North, where most of the nation's imports were consumed, while exempting the South and West. In effect, they said, the region that opposed the war was being saddled with taxes to pay for it. "Is it just and fair," asked a New York Federalist, "to aban-don the internal taxes and impose so much of the burden of the war upon the people of the northern and eastern states, the majority of whom are known to be opposed to it?"

Republicans turned a deaf ear to these protests. Instead, they met the revenue shortfall by relying on loans and interest-bearing treasury notes. Not until a year into the war did Congress finally impose the internal taxes that Gallatin had called for. These were supplemented by anoth-er round of excise taxes near the end of the war. Together, these duties constituted the most sweeping system of excise taxes enacted before the Civil War—far more sweeping than anything the Federalists had adopt-ed in the 1790s.

As comprehensive as this tax program was, it did not prevent the collapse of public credit in the summer of 1814. The government was unable to borrow the money it needed that year, and many contractors would no longer accept treasury notes. As a result, the government could not pay its bills or service the national debt. For all practical purposes, public credit was extinct, and the government was bankrupt.

The government's financial woes were further compounded by the suspension of specie payments. The banks outside of New England had issued so many notes during the war that in the summer of 1814 they stopped redeeming them in gold or silver. Once the banks went off a specie-paying basis, they stopped honoring each other's notes. This prevented the administration from using the banks to move funds across the country. It also reduced public revenue because the Treasury De-partment continued to accept depreciated bank paper at face value in the payment of taxes and the fulfillment of loan contracts.

Public finances were in such a chaotic state that in late 1814 the ad-ministration recommended the establishment of a national bank. His-torically the Republicans had opposed such a bank because they believed it was an engine of aristocracy that favored northern commercial inter-ests. But as the nation's financial situation deteriorated, Republican support for a bank steadily mounted. The various factions in Congress, however, could never agree on the details, and news of peace finally killed the proposal.

❖ ❖ ❖ ❖ ❖

The administration had to deal with another controversial issue during the war—the fate of the restrictive system. Although commercial sanctions always had been defended as an alternative to war—as a peaceful means of upholding the nation's rights—most Republicans were reluctant to give them up even after war had been declared. As Jefferson's secretary of state, Madison had been the chief architect of the restrictive system, and the war in no way dampened his ardor. Even some of the War Hawks shared his views. Six months into the war, Henry Clay conceded that the nation might be defeated in battle. "But if you cling to the restrictive system," he said, "it is incessantly working in your favor," and "if persisted in, the restrictive system, aiding the war, would break down the present [British] ministry, and lead to a consequent honorable peace."

Other Republicans, however, did not share this view. Langdon Cheves, a South Carolina War Hawk, claimed that the restrictive system "puts out one eye of your enemy, but it puts out both your own. It exhausts the purse, it exhausts the spirit, and paralyzes the sword of the nation." The ninety-day embargo and nonexportation law were due to expire in July of 1812, and Cheves urged Congress to repeal the nonimportation act of 1811 as well. Congress refused. This showed that the Republican majority was determined to use commercial restrictions as well as armed force to bring the British to terms.

Having resolved this problem, Congress turned to the closely related but complex issue of trading with the enemy. In spite of continued support for the restrictive system, there were many Americans, merchants and farmers alike, who opposed any additional legislation that would limit their wartime economic opportunities. Jefferson, for one, thought that the preservation of agricultural prosperity was vital to the success of the war policy. "To keep open sufficient markets," he told Madison, "is the very first object towards maintaining the popularity of the war."

In accordance with this thinking, Congress in the summer of 1812 passed an enemy trade act that prohibited commerce with the British Empire but did not bar American merchants from using British licenses to trade in non-British ports. This assured the continued shipment of American provisions to British troops on the European continent—a trade that had reached huge proportions and was of vital importance to the British.

Although the nonimportation law and the enemy trade act should have prevented direct trade with the British, the administration found it impossible to enforce these measures. On every frontier, trade with the enemy flourished despite the best efforts of customs agents and military officials to stop it.

On the Gulf Coast, the Baratarian pirates, who had established a settlement on Grand Terre Island in southern Louisiana, smuggled goods—British and non-British alike—into New Orleans. The smugglers operated openly and were welcomed by local merchants, who reaped huge profits. Local collusion was so widespread that government officials were helpless. "I will not dissemble," Secretary of the Navy William Jones told the New Orleans customs collector in 1813, "that whilst the inhabitants of Louisiana continue to countenance this illegal commerce and the courts of justice forbear to enforce the laws against the offenders, little or no benefit can be expected to result from the best concerted measures."

There was also extensive trade with the British along the Atlantic Coast. Amelia Island, a Spanish possession at the mouth of St. Marys River in Florida, was the principal outlet for southern produce and the main source of British goods for people living in the South. Shortly before the war, Gallatin received reports "that British goods to an immense amount have been imported into Amelia Island, with the view of smuggling the same into the United States."

Nor was the government able to keep provisions from British fleets in American waters. "The fact is notorious," declared the Lexington *Reporter*, "that the very squadrons of the enemy now annoying our coast . . . derive their supplies from the very country which is the theater of their atrocities." Admiralty procurers paid for provisions in cash, and there was no shortage of volunteers to supply their needs. Chesapeake Bay, Long Island Sound, and Vineyard Sound teemed with tiny coasters ferrying supplies to British fleets stationed there. Some sixty vessels were engaged in this traffic in Long Island Sound alone. Although most of this trade was clandestine, the harbor at Provincetown, Massachusetts, was openly used by British warships seeking provisions or refuge from winter storms. According to one report, small coasters and fishing vessels regularly carried "fresh beef, vegetables, and in fact all kind of supplies" to these ships.

The trade with Canada was even more extensive, and it increased rapidly to meet the needs of the growing British army there. The traffic was carried on overland, via inland waterways, and by the sea. "From the St. Lawrence to the ocean," reported an American army officer in 1814, "an open disregard prevails for the laws prohibiting intercourse with the enemy." As a result of this trade British troops feasted on American provisions. "Two-thirds of the army in Canada," Governor-General George Prevost boasted in August of 1814, "are at this moment eating beef provided by American contractors."

The illicit trade knew no political or social barriers. Federalists and Republicans alike profited from the trade, and local, state, and even federal officials often looked the other way. The trade gave a boost to local economies, a boost that was sorely needed because even though the middle and western states prospered during the war (mainly from army contracts), New England and the South suffered.

President Madison repeatedly asked Congress for new trade restrictions, both to put additional economic pressure on the British and to deny them access to goods that would assist them in prosecuting the war. Congress, however, rebuffed the president. Only reluctantly and after much acrimonious debate did Congress finally give the president the legislation he requested.

To supplement the nonimportation act of 1811 and the enemy trade act of 1812, Congress in the summer of 1813 passed a law barring the use of enemy licenses. Characteristically, however, this measure was adopted only after a federal court had ruled in the *Julia* case that an American ship sailing under a British license was a legitimate prize of war.

At the insistence of the president, Congress in December of 1813 enacted an embargo prohibiting American ships and goods from leaving port. This far-reaching law was really a coercive instrument in line with the old restrictive system. Its purpose was not so much to inhibit Britain's war effort as to put economic pressure on the British.

Shortly after the adoption of the embargo, news arrived that Napoleon had been defeated in the Battle of Leipzig. This opened all of northern Europe to British trade and thus deprived the restrictive system of much of its effectiveness as a coercive instrument. Under these circumstances, even President Madison had a change of heart, and in early 1814 he urged Congress to repeal the nonimportation law and the embargo. Although die-hard restrictionists were dismayed, Congress followed the president's lead and repealed both laws.

Since trade with the enemy—especially across the northern frontier—continued to mount, Congress in early 1815 enacted a new and sweeping enemy trade act that gave government officials more extensive powers than they had exercised under any previous trade restriction. This law, however, never was tested because it expired when peace was restored, two weeks after its adoption. Whether it would have worked may be doubted. The enforcement machinery of the customs department remained primitive, and people living on the frontiers showed a remarkable determination to keep profitable avenues of trade open.

❖ ❖ ❖ ❖ ❖

Besides recruiting men, raising money, and regulating trade with the enemy, the administration had to deal with another vexing problem. This was the treatment of prisoners of war. Although there was no international agreement on the subject, warfare in this era was carefully limited and highly professional, and each nation professed to favor humane treatment. The precedents, however, were vague, and prisoners on both sides complained of crowded, cold, and dirty housing, foul rations, and physical abuse.

Since officers were considered gentlemen, they received special treatment. Most were given the freedom of a town or larger area, and some were sent home on an extended parole, with the understanding that they would not fight again until officially exchanged. Members of the militia were sometimes sent home too, because they were considered part-time soldiers. Enlisted men, on the other hand, were usually confined until they were actually exchanged. The United States favored the use of state penitentiaries located near (but not too near) the northern frontier, particularly in Massachusetts and Kentucky. Great Britain, on the other hand, used a host of jails and prison ships scattered all over the Western world. The most notorious was Dartmoor, a cold, damp, and bleak prison located in England.

In principle men captured at sea were treated the same as those taken on land. Although the United States adhered to this principle, Great Britain did not. The British detained American seamen trapped in England by the war as well as those serving in the Royal Navy even though neither group qualified as prisoners of war. To deter privateering, the British also refused to exchange anyone taken from a privateer with fewer than fourteen guns. In addition, the British treated all maritime prisoners harshly, perhaps to show them the folly of making war on the Mistress of the Seas.

At first both sides adopted liberal parole policies for troops captured on the Canadian-American frontier, but this changed when a dispute arose over the treatment of prisoners of doubtful nationality. In the Battle of Queenston (fought in October of 1812), the British captured a large number of American soldiers, including twenty-three—mostly Irishmen—who had been born in the British Isles. Although some of these men were naturalized American citizens and others had lived in the United States for years, Royal officials considered them British subjects. They were consequently clamped in irons and shipped to England to be tried for treason.

The United States responded by ordering twenty-three British prisoners held in close confinement as hostages, and the British retaliated by confining forty-six American officers and noncommissioned officers. Retaliation continued on both sides, and by early 1814 all officers held as prisoners in the New World found themselves in close confinement, with the threat of retaliatory execution hanging over their heads.

Ultimately, good sense prevailed on both sides, and none of the confined prisoners was harmed. But this incident was not unique. On a number of occasions British officials learned that American prisoners they held had been born in the British Isles and threatened to try them for treason. In each case, however, the prospect of American retaliation forced them to relent.

❖ ❖ ❖ ❖ ❖

Yet another problem the administration had to contend with during the war was the opposition of the Federalists. This opposition, particularly in New England, was unrelenting and weighed heavily on the president's mind. "You are not mistaken," Madison wrote a friend in November of 1814, "in viewing the conduct of the eastern states as the source of our greatest difficulties in carrying on the war."

Ever since 1806 the Federalists had opposed the policy of confrontation with England—not only the loss of the Monroe-Pinkney Treaty but also the restrictive system and the drift toward war. One of the reasons that Republicans had gone to war in 1812 was to silence their critics. A state of war, they assumed, would force everyone—even Federalists—to rally to the flag. "A declaration of war," said New Hampshire Republican William Plumer, "must necessarily produce a great change in public opinion and the state of parties—British partisans must then either close their lips in silence or abscond."

As the nation moved toward war in early 1812, Republicans ominously hinted at what Federalists might expect if they did not cooperate. Once war is declared, said Tennessee War Hawk Felix Grundy in the halls of Congress, the only question would be "are you for your country or against it." Whenever that decision is made, echoed the semiofficial Washington *National Intelligencer,* "he that is not for us must be considered as against us and treated accordingly."

Many of these pleas—either openly or implicitly—carried a threat of violence. In a letter written to President Madison shortly after the declaration of war, Thomas Jefferson said, "The Federalists . . . are poor devils here, not worthy of notice. A barrel of tar to each state south of the Potomac will keep all in order, and that will be freely contributed without troubling government. To the north they will give you more trouble. You may there have to apply the rougher drastics of . . . hemp and confiscation." Jefferson might have been speaking half in jest, but other Republicans took the matter more seriously. Most saw the war in the same light that the Boston *Yankee* did—as a way to "ensure peace at home, if not with the world."

This intolerance led to violence against Federalists in the early months of the war. In Baltimore a series of grisly riots destroyed the offices of a Federalist newspaper and left one Federalist dead and several others crippled. Mobs also drove Federalist newspapers out of business in Savannah, Georgia, and Norristown, Pennsylvania, and other editors in the middle and southern states complained that they too had been warned to change their tune or risk a similar fate. "The war," said a Federalist newspaper, "pretendedly for the freedom of the seas, is valiantly waged against the freedom of the press."

Although some Federalists had initially talked of supporting the war, this sentiment quickly evaporated in the wake of the violence. In addition, Federalists were dismayed by the failure to limit the war to the high seas and to include France in the reprisals; by the retention of the restrictive system; and by the discriminatory tax program adopted. Convinced that the war was a party war that would do the nation far more harm than good, Federalists denounced the contest as unnecessary, unwise, and unjust. "Whether we consider our agriculture, our commerce, our monied systems, or our internal safety," concluded a Federalist newspaper in Virginia, "nothing but disaster can result from it."

The best way to bring the war to an end, most Federalists agreed, was to oppose it. Hence they wrote, spoke, and preached against the war; they discouraged enlistments in the army and subscriptions to the war loans; and they vigorously condemned all who supported the war and worked for their defeat at the polls.

In Congress Federalists voted as a bloc on all war legislation. They unanimously opposed the declaration of war in June of 1812, and thereafter they voted against almost every proposal to recruit troops, raise money, foster privateering, or restrict trade with the enemy. The only measures they supported were those they considered defensive—mainly bills to increase the navy or to build coastal fortifications.

Federalists in New England went further. Many shared an abhorrence of the war—often grounded on religious principles—that was unmatched elsewhere. "Each man who volunteers his services in such a cause," said a Massachusetts preacher, "or loans his money for its support, or by his conversation, his writings, or any other mode of influence, encourages its prosecution . . . loads his conscience with the blackest crimes."

Because they were the dominant party in New England, Federalists there did not have to worry about persecution or violence. They could also use the machinery of state and local government to publicize their opposition and obstruct the war effort. In Hartford, Connecticut, Federalists sought to end loud demonstrations by army recruiters by adopting city ordinances that restricted public music and parades. In New Bedford, Massachusetts, Federalists denounced privateering and voted to quarantine all arriving privateers for forty days—ostensibly on medical grounds but actually to protest the war.

New England Federalists made their opposition felt in other ways. After a Republican newspaper in Massachusetts denounced Federalists for applauding naval victories in a war they opposed, the state senate adopted a resolution declaring that "in a war like the present . . . it is not becoming a moral and religious people to express any approbation of military or naval exploits which are not immediately connected with the defense of our seacoast and soil." In early 1814 Massachusetts also refused to allow the federal government to continue to use its jails for prisoners of war.

❖ ❖ ❖ ❖ ❖

The most persistent source of conflict between New England and the federal government was over the deployment and control of the militia. This was no small matter because the New England militia was among the best in the nation, and most Federalists saw the militia as their best if not their only means of defense.

The first clash occurred in the summer of 1812, when the administration asked Massachusetts, Connecticut, and Rhode Island to call out militia to garrison coastal fortifications in the region. The governors of all three states refused, claiming that there was no real danger and that they could not place their militia under regular army officers anyway. The three governors refused to comply with the administration's request, both to protest the war and to ensure that they retain control over their militia. Already citizen soldiers from New York, Pennsylvania, and the western states were being marched to the Canadian frontier, and New Englanders feared that their militia would meet the same fate.

When the British actually threatened, however, the New England governors willingly called out their militia. They also tried to resolve their command problem with the federal government, though without much success. Since the federal government refused to supply or pay militia that were not placed under United States officers, Massachusetts, Connecticut, and Rhode Island had to finance their own defense measures in the last months of the war.

These costs steadily mounted, eventually reaching $850,000 in Massachusetts, $150,000 in Connecticut, and $50,000 in Rhode Island. Raising money to meet these costs was no easy task. New taxes were especially unpalatable because the federal burden was heavy and growing, and the entire region was in the throes of a wartime depression. Nor could the banks help. The suspension of specie payments elsewhere in the Union had forced New England banks to cut back on their loans in order to maintain their cash reserves.

❖ ❖ ❖ ❖ ❖

The defense problem was New England's chief grievance in 1814, but it was only a symptom of Federalist disillusionment over a broad range of Republican domestic and foreign policies. Equally disheartening, New England Federalists could see little prospect of winning control of the national government to effect any changes. In spite of the Federalists' wartime election gains, the Virginia dynasty remained firmly in control. In addition, the Louisiana Purchase had brought vast new territories under American control in 1803, and the flood of immigration (which was only temporarily halted by the war) promised to populate these territories with Republican voters.

Traditionally, Americans had dealt with crises by calling a convention. The Albany Congress (1754), the Stamp Act Congress (1765), the First Continental Congress (1774), and the Philadelphia Constitutional Convention (1787) were all convened to deal with crises. To address the crisis they faced in 1814, New England Federalists summoned the Hartford Convention.

The Hartford Convention met in secret from December 15, 1814, to January 5, 1815. Although some Federalist newspapers talked boldly of signing a separate peace and seceding from the Union, the Hartford Convention was firmly under the control of moderates. The report of the convention, which was largely the work of Harrison Gray Otis of Massachusetts, clearly reflected this moderation.

About half of the report was devoted to immediate concerns related to the war: the defense problem and the threat that Congress would resort to conscription. To finance local defense measures, the report advised the states to seek authority from the national government to use federal tax money collected within their borders. To deal with unconstitutional measures for raising troops, the report (in its only radical proposal) recommended nullification, asserting that is was the duty of a state "to interpose its authority" to protect its citizens.

The rest of the report was devoted to long-term problems. To remedy these, the report recommended seven constitutional amendments calling for a two-thirds vote in Congress to declare war, restrict trade, or admit new states to the Union; a sixty-day limit on embargoes; an end to the constitutional rule that counted three-fifths of slaves in apportioning representation in Congress; a ban against naturalized citizens' holding federal office; and a provision that would limit presidents to one term and bar the election of a president from the same state twice in a row.

These amendments represented a catalogue of New England's grievances over the years. They struck at the restrictive system and the war, the overrepresentation of white southerners in Congress, the growing political power of the West, the influence of foreign-born officeholders (such as Swiss-born Albert Gallatin), and the domination of the Virginia dynasty. Federalists hoped that the adoption of these amendments would restore sectional balance and prevent a renewal of those policies that had been most injurious to New England.

Massachusetts and Connecticut approved the amendments and sent emissaries to Washington to secure federal tax money for defense measures. On their way the envoys learned of Andrew Jackson's victory at New Orleans, and news of peace soon followed. The envoys were the butt of much Republican humor, and nothing came of their mission.

The Hartford Convention was the climax of Federalist opposition to the war. Although it represented a triumph for moderation, few people remembered it that way in the rush of events at the end of the war. Instead, the Hartford Convention became a synonym for treason, and Federalists were blamed for all the shortcomings of the war. People forgot that both parties were involved in the inner war and that Republicans no less than Federalists deserved a share of the blame for the nation's misfortunes.

6

THE PEACE OF CHRISTMAS EVE

In the military and naval campaigns, the record of the United States during the War of 1812 was decidedly mixed. There were some successes—most notably on the northern lakes and at New Orleans—and some failures—particularly in the Chesapeake Bay and on the Canadian frontier. In the peace negotiations, however, the nation's record was much better, not because of what the diplomats won but because of what they avoided losing. No single campaign in the field loomed as large as these negotiations. It was here—in Ghent, Belgium, rather than on the battlefield—that the United States consistently outmaneuvered the enemy, and it was here that Americans could claim their most significant victory.

American success at the negotiating table was fitting because it was here that Republicans expected to win the war. Some Republicans—the "scarecrow" party—had supported military preparations in the War Congress in the hope of persuading the British to make concessions. When this failed, some voted for the declaration of war for the same reason. Although most Republicans believed that the conquest of Canada would be a mere matter of marching, many hoped that no marching would be necessary—that the decision for war itself would be enough to win concessions from the enemy. In this sense, the declaration of war was a bluff designed to force the British to take American demands seriously.

That the president himself harbored these views is suggested by the haste with which he sent out peace feelers in the early days of the war. "The sword was scarcely out of the scabbard," Madison said, "before the enemy was apprised of the reasonable terms on which it would be resheathed." Madison outlined his terms to departing British minister Augustus J. Foster, and Secretary of State James Monroe urged Foster to work for peace.

The administration also pursued peace through Jonathan Russell, its diplomatic representative in London. On June 26, barely a week after the declaration of war, the State Department dispatched a note to Russell authorizing him to sign an armistice if the British would give up the Orders in Council and impressment. By the time Russell made this offer in late August, the Orders in Council already had been repealed. This left impressment as the only issue that stood in the way of peace.

The British, however, showed no interest in Russell's offer. Having made one important concession—on the Orders in Council—they were in no mood to make another. With the war only a few weeks old, the British foreign secretary, Lord Castlereagh, expressed surprise at America's eagerness for peace. "If the American government was so anxious *to get rid of the war*," he told Russell, "it would have an opportunity of doing so on learning the revocation of the Orders in Council."

The British did not doubt that the repeal of the Orders in Council would end the war. For years British restrictions on neutral trade had been the leading source of Anglo-American friction, while impressment had not been a major issue since the loss of the Monroe-Pinkney Treaty and the *Chesapeake* affair in 1807. Convinced that peace would soon be restored, the British waited until October 13—ten weeks after receiving the news of war—before authorizing general reprisals against the United States.

In the meantime, the British government instructed its representatives in the American theater to propose a cease-fire. Officials in Canada responded by signing an armistice with General Henry Dearborn. The American government, however, repudiated the agreement because it did not provide for an end to impressment. The negotiations in 1812 consequently ended in failure, even though both sides were interested in peace.

❖ ❖ ❖ ❖ ❖

In March of 1813 Andrei Dashkov, the Russian minister in Washington, invited the United States to take part in a new round of negotiations, this time under the auspices of his government. The administration welcomed the Russian offer. Russia had long championed neutral rights, and American officials expected to profit from its mediation. "There is not a single [maritime] interest," Monroe said, "in which Russia and the other Baltic powers may not be considered as having a common interest with the United States."

American officials were anxious for peace for several reasons. The campaign against Canada had not gone well, Federalist opposition to the war remained adamant, and the nation's financial situation was already deteriorating. Furthermore, Napoleon's retreat from Russia had greatly strengthened Britain's hand on the continent. If France was defeated, the United States might find itself alone in the field against Britain. To avoid this prospect, American officials hoped to liquidate the war in the New World while Britain was still tied up in the Old World.

Without waiting for Britain's response to the Russian offer, Madison chose three peace commissioners and dispatched them to Europe. Albert Gallatin, who had grown weary of his duties at the Treasury Department, was chosen to head the mission. He was joined by John Quincy Adams, the American minister in St. Petersburg, and James A. Bayard, a moderate Delaware Federalist. The Senate rejected Gallatin's nomination because he was still a member of the cabinet, but by this time he was already in Europe.

The instructions the commissioners carried with them called for British concessions on a broad range of maritime issues and the surrender of Canada as well. Only one demand, however, was a *sine qua non*—a point deemed essential to any settlement—and that was an end to impressment.

Gallatin and Bayard joined Adams in St. Petersburg in July of 1813. There they attended an unending round of parties, while waiting for Britain's official response to the mediation offer. In fact, the British already had rejected the proposal. They had no desire (as Castlereagh put it) to allow the United States "to mix directly or indirectly her maritime interests with those of another state"—certainly not with those of a great inland power that favored a broad definition of neutral rights.

❖   ❖   ❖   ❖   ❖

Although British officials rejected the Russian offer, they felt obliged to make a counteroffer to demonstrate their peaceful intentions. Having already raised the possibility of direct talks through various other channels, Castlereagh sent a message to Monroe in November of 1813 offering "to enter upon a direct negotiation for the restoration of peace." Castlereagh strongly hinted, however, that the British would not give up impressment.

President Madison accepted this offer and appointed four men to serve on the commission. Adams was chosen to head the mission. The other members were Bayard, Kentucky War Hawk Henry Clay, and Jonathan Russell, who had conducted the early armistice negotiations in London. Three weeks later, when Madison learned that Gallatin was still in Europe, his name was added to the list. This time the president mollified the Senate by appointing a new secretary of the treasury. This assured Senate approval for Gallatin's nomination.

The American commission was exceptionally strong. Four of the envoys already had distinguished themselves in public life, and Adams and Clay still had long and important careers ahead of them. Only Russell would never achieve any great distinction. With such a strong mission, differences of opinion were inevitable. Clay and Adams were frequently at odds, though usually on minor issues. "Upon almost all the important questions," Adams said, "we have been unanimous."

The British appointed their envoys in May of 1814, just after the end of the European war. In contrast to the United States, Britain had to rely on second-rate men because its top officials would be busy trying to forge a European peace settlement at the Congress of Vienna. The British peace mission consisted of Dr. William Adams, an admiralty lawyer; Lord Gambier, a veteran naval officer; and Henry Goulburn, an undersecretary in the Colonial Office. Goulburn was the most ambitious and energetic of the three, and he took charge of the negotiations.

The British envoys were slow to depart for Ghent because British officials hoped that victories in America would enhance their bargaining position. Now that the war in Europe was over, the mood in England was vindictive. "War with America, and most inveterate war," said a friendly Englishman, "is in the mouth of almost everyone you meet in this wise and thinking nation."

American officials had hoped that the great powers on the Continent would serve as a counterpoise to British strength, but it soon became apparent that British influence was everywhere paramount. Nevertheless, everyone—the British included—recognized that the American war hampered Britain's freedom of action on the Continent, and as time passed, sympathy for the United States mounted. The United States profited from this undercurrent of sympathy. Despite

British protests, French officials continued to allow American privateers to cruise from their ports even though France was no longer at war with England.

❖ ❖ ❖ ❖ ❖

The peace negotiations were originally planned for Gothenburg, Sweden, but the end of the war in Europe made Ghent more convenient because it afforded quicker access to both capitals. The negotiations lasted from August 8, 1814, to December 24, 1814—far longer than anyone expected though not as long as the Congress of Vienna, which met from September 1814 to June 1815.

When the negotiations began, the American envoys were still bound to insist on an end to impressment. Like other American diplomats in this era, they were prepared to violate their instructions if they had to. This was unnecessary, however, because in June of 1814 the administration, realizing the hopelessness its position, decided to drop impressment. The new instructions reached the envoys just as the negotiations got under way.

With impressment out of the way, the envoys were able to focus on other issues. In the first two weeks of the negotiations the British presented their terms. As a *sine qua non* for peace, they insisted that the western Indians be included in the settlement and that a permanent reservation be established for them in the Old Northwest. In addition, the British demanded territory in northern Maine (to facilitate overland traffic between Quebec and Halifax) and in present-day Minnesota (to assure access to the Mississippi River). They also called on the United States to demilitarize the Great Lakes—removing all warships from those waters and all fortifications from the shores. Finally, the British declared that the American right to fish in Canadian waters and to dry their catch on Canadian shores would not be renewed without an equivalent.

The British terms were based on several considerations, but uppermost was their concern for Canadian security. It was "notorious to the whole world," the British envoys said, "that the conquest of Canada and its permanent annexation to the United States was the declared object of the American government." The British were also anxious to protect their Indian allies, whom they had abandoned in the Peace of Paris in 1783 and again in the Jay Treaty of 1794.

The British suggested as a boundary for the Indian reservation the line established by the Treaty of Greenville in 1795, though subject to "such modifications as might be agreed upon." This treaty had been superseded by others, but if resurrected, it would have secured to the Indians about a third of Ohio, half of Minnesota, and almost all of Indiana, Illinois, Michigan, and Wisconsin.

This territory was not, as the American envoys claimed, a third of the land mass of the United States, but 250,000 square miles, or about 15 percent. The region was inhabited by some 20,000 Indians and about 100,000 whites. When asked what would become of those whites who found themselves on the wrong side of the new boundary, the British replied that "they must shift for themselves"—meaning that they would have to abandon their homes.

The British terms need not have surprised anyone since they had been anticipated by newspaper articles on both sides of the Atlantic. Nevertheless, the American envoys were stunned. Although aware of the strident anti-American feeling in England, they had assumed that the British government would be more conciliatory. They failed to realize that with the war in Europe over, British leaders were anxious to end the American war on terms that would ensure that Canada and its Indian allies would be amply protected in the future.

The American envoys flatly rejected the British terms. "A treaty concluded upon such terms," they said, "would be but an armistice. It cannot be supposed that America would long submit to conditions so injurious and degrading." The Indian reservation was particularly objectionable. It undermined American sovereignty, ran counter to a tradition of national control over the Indians, and threatened the westward movement.

With the talks apparently stalled, the mood of the American envoys darkened. Only Clay retained even a shred of hope for peace. An inveterate gambler who sometimes stayed up all night playing cards, Clay thought the British might be bluffing. The Kentucky War Hawk found it difficult to believe that the British would allow the talks to break up over the issues in question. "Such a rupture," he said, "would entirely change the whole character of the war, would unite all parties at home, and would organize a powerful opposition in Great Britain."

Clay's suspicions were well founded. The British demands were what one scholar has called "a probing operation." Their purpose was to provide a basis for negotiation and to determine what concessions the Americans were willing to make. Even the Indian reservation was not supposed to be a *sine qua non,* although the British envoys mistakenly had presented it as one.

Unwilling to end the negotiations, the British gradually retreated from their demands. Instead of an Indian reservation, they agreed to settle for a pledge to restore the Indians to their status as of 1811. This stipulation was too vague to be meaningful. For all practical purposes, the British once again had abandoned their Indian allies.

Having retreated from their initial terms, the British offered a new basis for peace in October—*uti possidetis,* which meant that each side would retain whatever territory it held at the time the treaty was signed. If this offer was accepted, the British would gain eastern Maine, Mackinac, and Fort Niagara, while the United States would get Fort Malden and Fort Erie.

The British suggested that the agreement be "subject to such modifications as mutual convenience may be found to require." Their hope was to retain northern Maine (for the overland route between Quebec and Halifax) as well as Mackinac and Fort Niagara and to trade the rest of eastern Maine for forts Malden and Erie. The British gave little thought to the possibility of retaining New Orleans because by this time their projected campaign against the Crescent City played only a minor role in their overall strategy for ending the war.

When it became evident that the Americans would not agree to *uti possidetis,* the British dropped this demand just as they had dropped their others. By this time the shrill attacks against the United States in the British press had given way to protests over war taxes. "Economy and relief from taxation are not merely the war cry of opposition," said one official, "but they are the real objects to which public attention is turned."

The British were also disillusioned by the lack of military progress in America. Reports of the fall of Washington and the occupation of eastern Maine had raised their hopes, but news of the failures at Baltimore and Plattsburgh soon followed. Their counteroffensive in 1814 was proving far less successful than they had anticipated.

Another year of fighting was also likely to undermine Britain's position in Europe. The allies at Vienna were already quarreling among themselves, and British officials were wondering how quickly they could recall troops from America. "The negotiations at Vienna are not proceeding in the way we could wish," said the British prime minister, Lord Liverpool, "and this consideration itself was deserving of some weight in deciding the question of peace with America."

To buttress their position at home and in the field, British officials asked the Duke of Wellington to take charge of the American war. The Iron Duke agreed but refused to leave Europe until the spring or to guarantee success. "I feel no objection to going to America," he told Liverpool, "though I don't promise to myself much success there." What the British needed was "not a general, or general officers and troops, but a naval superiority on the lakes." Without this, there was little hope of success. Given the existing circumstances, Wellington concluded, "you have no right . . . to demand any concession of territory from America."

Wellington's opinion was all that British officials needed to jettison their last territorial demands. The only important issues that remained unsettled were the status of American fishing rights in Canadian waters and British navigation rights on the Mississippi River. Since both rights were guaranteed by the Treaty of 1783, both were likely to stand or fall together.

These rights caused a deeper division in the American delegation than any other issue had. Clay, representing western interests, wanted to close the Mississippi to the British, while Adams, representing Massachusetts fishermen, insisted on retaining the fisheries. Ultimately, both issues were left out of the treaty. This was a tacit admission that both rights continued, which was a victory for Adams.

The American and British envoys spent close to a month hammering the treaty into final form. Their handiwork—completed on December 24, 1814—is known as the Treaty of Ghent or the Peace of Christmas Eve. The treaty mentioned none of the maritime issues that had caused the war. It simply restored the *status quo ante bellum*—the state that existed before the war. Each nation also promised to make peace with the Indians and "to restore to such tribes . . . all the possessions, rights, and privileges which they may have enjoyed, or been entitled to," in 1811. In addition, the treaty established commissions—three in all—to fix the Canadian-American boundary, which was disputed in several places. Both nations also promised to "use their best endeavors" to stamp out the slave trade.

On three earlier occasions—in connection with the Jay Treaty in 1794, a boundary convention in 1803, and the Monroe-Pinkney Treaty in 1806—the United States had insisted on modifications after an agreement had been signed by its envoys. This time the British made it clear they would settle for nothing less than unconditional ratification. They also insisted that hostilities cease not when the agreement was signed (which was customary) but only after both sides had ratified it.

❖ ❖ ❖ ❖ ❖

On January 2, 1815, Henry Carroll, Clay's personal secretary, boarded the ship *Favourite* in London to take a copy of the treaty to the United States. He was joined by Anthony Baker, who carried a copy of the British instrument of ratification. The ship encountered bad weather in the Chesapeake Bay and hence headed for New York Harbor, docking around 8:00 P.M. on February 11. Carroll made no secret of his mission. Word quickly spread that peace was at hand, and soon the entire city was celebrating.

From New York, reports of the treaty spread in all directions. An express rider carried the news to Boston in a record thirty-two hours. Handbills announcing the treaty were distributed throughout the city. Schools were closed, people left their jobs, and the legislature adjourned. In the boisterous celebration that followed, bells were rung, the city was illuminated, troops turned out to fire a salute, and cartmen formed a procession of sleighs, parading around the city with the word "peace" on their hats.

Celebrations of this sort took place all over the country. "Grand illuminations are making throughout the United States," said one American. Everywhere, too, the news of peace drove up the price of war bonds and treasury notes. Goods that were normally shipped to foreign markets also rose in value, while war materiel and imported goods declined.

The British were prepared to offer a separate peace to New England if the treaty was not ratified, but there was no danger of this happening. Madison submitted the treaty to the Senate on February 15, and the next day the Senate voted unanimously (35 to 0) to approve it. Madison gave his own approval later that day, thus completing the ratification process. Since the British had already ratified, this marked the end of hostilities. The war formally came to an end at 11:00 P.M. the following day—February 17—when Monroe exchanged ratifications with Baker, who had arrived in Washington earlier that evening.

Although Americans of both political parties rejoiced at the restoration of peace, Federalists had special cause to celebrate. The war, after all, had achieved none of the nation's maritime goals. Instead, the Treaty of Ghent seemed to confirm what Federalists had been saying all along about the futility of the conflict.

Many Federalists expected to reap significant political dividends, but James Robertson of Philadelphia was not so optimistic. The Republicans, he said, would ignore the causes of the conflict and portray it as "a war on our part of pure self-defense against the designs of the British to reduce us again to [colonial] subjection." By portraying the war in this light, they could claim that it was a great triumph. "The President," Robertson concluded, "will only have to call it a glorious peace, and the party here will echo it."

Robertson's prophecy proved correct. In a message to Congress announcing the end of the war, President Madison congratulated Americans "upon an event which is highly honorable to the nation, and terminates, with peculiar felicity, a campaign signalized by the most brilliant successes." The war, Madison claimed, "has been waged with a success which is the natural result of the wisdom of the legislative councils, of the patriotism of the people, of the public spirit of the militia, and of the valor of the military and naval forces of the country."

All across the country Republican orators and editors echoed the president's cry. "This second war of independence," crowed the New York *National Advocate*, "has been illustrated by more splendid achievements than the war of the revolution." The nation had attained all of its objectives, added a writer for the *National Intelligencer:* "The administration has succeeded in asserting the principles of God and nature against the encroachments of human ambition and tyranny."

The Republicans exaggerated, for in spite of the victories achieved in the last year of the contest, the United States could not in good conscience claim to have won the war. But because of the clear-headed determination shown by its envoys at Ghent, the nation could at least claim it had won the peace.

CONCLUSION

The War of 1812 is often called America's "second war of independence."
The issues and ideology of this conflict did echo those of the Revolu-
tion, but the supposed threat to American independence in 1812 was
more imagined than real. It existed mainly in the minds of thin-skinned
Republicans who were unable to shed the ideological legacy of the
Revolution and interpreted all British actions accordingly.

There is no denying that British encroachments on American rights
were both real and serious. Throughout this period, however, the focus
of British policy was always on Europe. The overriding objective of the
British government was to secure the defeat of France, and all else was
subordinated to this purpose. Britain's aim, in other words, was not to
subvert American independence but to win the war in Europe. Once this
objective was achieved, its infringements on American rights would cease.

Not only did Republicans misread British intentions, but throughout this turbulent era they consistently overrated America's ability to
win concessions. "We have considered ourselves of too much importance in the scale of nations," Daniel Sheffey, a Virginia Federalist, said.
"It has led us into great errors. Instead of yielding to circumstances,
which human power cannot control, we have imagined that our own
destiny, and that of other nations, was in our hands, to be regulated as
we thought proper." Sheffey's analysis was borne out, not only by the
restrictive system but also by the war.

❖　❖　❖　❖　❖

The War of 1812 lasted only two years and eight months—from June
18, 1812, to February 17, 1815. Though the war was not long, the United

States was beset by problems from the beginning. Many of the nation's military leaders were incompetent, and enlistments in the army and navy lagged behind need. The militia was costly and inefficient and repeatedly refused to cross into Canada or to hold its position under enemy fire. In addition, the government found it difficult to borrow money, and the nation's finances became increasingly chaotic. There was also extensive trade with the enemy, trade in which Federalists and Republicans alike freely took part. A combination of Federalist opposition, Republican factionalism, and general public apathy undermined the entire war effort.

Congress was partly responsible for this state of affairs. Endless debate and deep divisions delayed or prevented the adoption of much-needed legislation. Congress was particularly negligent on financial matters. Hoping for a quick war and fearing the political consequences of unpopular measures, Republicans postponed internal taxes and delayed a national bank. As a result, public credit collapsed in 1814, and a general suspension of specie payments ensued. If the contest had continued much longer, the Revolutionary War phrase "not worth a continental" might have been replaced by "not worth a treasury note."

A strong president might have overcome some of these problems, but Madison was one of the weakest war leaders in the nation's history. Although his opponents called the contest "Mr. Madison's War," it never bore his stamp. Cautious, shy, and circumspect, Madison was unable to supply the bold and vigorous leadership that was needed. "Mr. Madison is wholly unfit for the storms of war," Henry Clay observed. "Nature has cast him in too benevolent a mould."

In some respects, to be sure, Madison's caution served the nation well. Unlike other war presidents, he showed remarkable respect for the civil rights of his domestic foes. Despite pleas from other Republicans, he refused to resort to a sedition law. Even though Federalists had to face mob violence (particularly at the beginning of the war), they never had to contend with government repression. Madison's treatment of prisoners of war was also commendably humane, and his circumspect policy on disaffection in New England was undoubtedly well judged too.

In other ways, however, Madison's cautious brand of leadership undermined the nation's war effort. He allowed such incompetents as William Eustis and Paul Hamilton to hold key positions, and he tolerated intrigues and backbiting among his closest advisers. Madison was also slow to get rid of incompetent generals in the field and to promote officers who had proven themselves in battle. Because he lacked a commanding influence in Congress, he was unable to secure vital legislation, and because he lacked a strong following in the country, he was unable to inspire people to open their hearts and purses.

No doubt poor leadership in Washington and in the field drove up the cost of this war. The battle casualties were comparatively light: 2,260 killed and 4,505 wounded. The number of nonbattle deaths—mostly from disease—was probably about 17,000. The army executed an additional 205 men, mainly for repeated desertion, and the navy executed a few men too. Some men who had served on privateers also died in the war, primarily from disease in British prisons. There were a few civilian casualties as well—mostly victims of Indian raids in the West. In all, the number of American deaths attributable to the war was probably about 20,000.

The financial cost of the war (excluding property damage, lost economic opportunities, and land bounties) was $158 million. This includes $93 million in army and navy expenditures, $16 million for interest on the war loans, and $49 million in veterans' benefits. (The last veteran died in 1905, the last pensioner—the daughter of a veteran—in 1946.) The national debt, which Republicans had reduced from $83 million in 1801 to $45 million in 1812, soared to $127 million by the end of 1815.

❖ ❖ ❖ ❖ ❖

What did the war accomplish? Although militarily the conflict ended in a draw, in a larger sense it represented a failure for Republican policymakers. The nation was unable to conquer Canada or to achieve any of its maritime goals. Indeed, these issues were not even mentioned in the peace treaty, which merely provided for restoring all conquered territory and returning to the *status quo ante bellum*.

In other ways, however, the war was fraught with consequences. The United States annexed part of Spanish West Florida in 1813—the only permanent land acquisition made during the war, though it came at the expense of a neutral power rather than the enemy.

The war also broke the power of the Indians in the Old West. The attempts of Tecumseh and the Prophet in the Northwest and of the Red Sticks in the Southwest to halt the tide of American expansion ended in failure. Instead, the Indian wars gave the United States government both the excuse and the incentive to accelerate the forced removal of the eastern tribes to lands beyond the Mississippi River. Never again would Indians seriously threaten the United States, and never again would a foreign nation tamper with American Indians. The subjugation of the Indians, in turn, promoted manifest destiny and the westward movement. The heady nationalism and expansionism that characterized American foreign policy throughout the nineteenth century was at least partly a result of the War of 1812.

Even though the war stimulated nationalism, it was also an important benchmark in the history of American sectionalism. To retain control of their militia and obstruct war measures, New England Federalists resurrected the states' rights doctrine that Virginia Republicans had used in the late 1790s to fight the alien and sedition laws. This same doctrine would later flourish in the South, until a northern victory in the Civil War delivered a body blow to the whole notion of states' rights.

The war also stimulated peacetime defense spending. In his message to Congress announcing the end of hostilities, President Madison echoed an old Federalist plea by calling for preparedness. "Experience has taught us," he said, "that a certain degree of preparation for war is not only indispensable to avert disasters in the onset, but affords also the best security for the continuance of peace." Congress agreed. The peacetime army was fixed at 10,000 men in 1815 (three times what it had been in 1802), and the construction of nine ships-of-the-line and twelve heavy frigates was authorized in 1816. Congress also launched a far-reaching program to fortify the coast, appropriating almost $8.5 million for this purpose between 1816 and 1829.

The war affected the American military establishment in another way. Those officers who had outlived their usefulness—Alexander Smyth, James Wilkinson, Wade Hampton, and the like—were cast aside during the war to make room for younger men, such as Jacob Brown, Winfield Scott, Edmund Gaines, Alexander Macomb, and Andrew Jackson. As a result, the American army had a decidedly new look by 1815. Some navy officers also burned their names into the history books. Among these were Oliver Perry, Thomas Macdonough, Isaac Hull, William Bainbridge, Stephen Decatur, and Charles Stewart.

The war had a dramatic impact on the American economy too. Unlike most American wars, this one did not generate a general economic boom. According to Thomas Jefferson, whose heavy debts became unmanageable during the war, the conflict "arrested the course of the most remarkable tide of prosperity any nation ever experienced." Although people in the middle and western states prospered, those in

New England and the South did not. Manufacturing thrived because of the absence of British competition, but whatever gains were made in this sector of the economy were dwarfed by heavy losses in fishing and commerce. For most Americans, the economic opportunities were greater before and after the war than during it.

The war left an enduring legacy of Anglophobia in the United States. Hatred of England, originally kindled by the American Revolution, was further inflamed by the War of 1812—particularly by the Indian atrocities in the West and British depredations in the Chesapeake.

Britain's treatment of American prisoners of war further intensified this Anglophobia. At one time or another about 20,000 Americans, mostly men who had served on privateers, were held in British prisons. British officials often treated these prisoners roughly. Even before the war was over, stories of abuse began to filter back to the United States. After the war ended, the trickle of stories became a torrent. "The return of our people from British prisons," said *Niles' Register*, "have filled the newspapers with tales of horror."

Some of the stories came from Halifax, where most Americans captured on the northern frontier were held. "All the prisoners that we have yet seen," said the Boston *Patriot*, "agree that their treatment in the Halifax prisons was brutal and barbarous in the extreme."

Other stories came from Dartmoor, a damp and dreary prison in southwestern England. By the end of the war, "this accursed place," as one prisoner called it, housed some 5,000 Americans. Trouble at Dartmoor reached a climax on April 6, 1815—almost two months after the war ended—when a dispute over responsibility for transporting the men home delayed repatriation. Anxious to regain their freedom, the prisoners became unruly, and British soldiers fired on them, killing six and wounding sixty others.

Americans did not soon forget the brutality of the war. As early as 1813, the House of Representatives published a study—with extensive documentation—that criticized Great Britain for the Indian atrocities, the Chesapeake depredations, and the mistreatment of prisoners. Other stories kept the embers of hatred alive for decades. Long after the conflict was over, *Niles' Register* published war-related anecdotes and documents that showed the British in a bad light, and some nineteenth-century histories continued this tradition by focusing on Britain's misdeeds.

Another legacy of the war was the enhanced reputation that the

United States enjoyed in Europe. Although America's performance in the war was mixed, it earned the respect of Europe. "The Americans," said Augustus J. Foster, "have had the satisfaction of proving their courage—they have brought us to speak of them with respect."

The British were careful not to impress any Americans when the Royal Navy went back on a war footing during Napoleon's Hundred Days in 1815. In fact, Americans were never again subjected to those dubious maritime practices that had caused the war. With Europe generally at peace in the century after Waterloo, the Great Powers had no interest in regulating America's trade or tampering with its merchant marine. The United States had ample time to grow and to husband its strength so that it could meet the Great Powers on an equal footing in the next great conflict—World War I.

The war also left an enduring political legacy. Some statesmen—James Monroe, Andrew Jackson, John Quincy Adams, and William Henry Harrison—were able to parlay their public service during the war into the presidency. A host of lesser lights also made political capital out of the war. The Battle of the Thames, which became a kind of Bunker Hill in western legend, helped create one president, one vice president, three governors, three lieutenant governors, four senators, and twenty congressmen.

The war confirmed Republican dominance and brought the first party system to an end. The Republicans laid claim to all the victories in the war and blamed the defeats on the Federalists. The Republicans also charged the Federalists with prolonging the war, though the available evidence suggests that opposition in both countries shortened the conflict by making each government more amenable to a compromise peace.

What did the Federalists reap from their opposition to the war? Nothing that was good. Although individual Federalists—such as John Marshall, Daniel Webster, and Josiah Quincy—continued to be active in public life, the party itself never overcame the taint of treason. Opposition to the war was popular during the conflict but not afterward, and Federalists found it particularly difficult to live down the notoriety of the Hartford Convention.

Federalists protested that they were made the scapegoats for the failure of Republican policies. "The charge that opposition encourages the enemy and injures the cause," said Senator Rufus King of New York, "has at all times been made as an excuse for the failure and defeat of a weak administration." These protests fell on deaf ears. The decline of the Federalist party—begun in 1800 but arrested by the restrictive system and the war—continued apace after the war was over.

It mattered not that the war had vindicated so many Federalist policies—particularly the importance of military and naval preparedness and the need for internal taxes and a national bank—and that Republicans themselves admitted as much by adopting these policies during or after the war. It mattered not that Federalists had predicted the futility of the conflict and that the Treaty of Ghent had proven them right. What mattered was that the nation had emerged from the war without surrendering any rights or territory and with just enough triumphs—on both land and sea—to give the appearance of victory.

The Battle of New Orleans, though fought after Great Britain had signed and ratified the peace treaty, played a particularly important role in forging the myth of American victory. Even before the peace terms were known, Republicans were touting this battle as a decisive turning point in the war. "The terms of the treaty are yet unknown to us," said Congressman Charles J. Ingersoll in early 1815. "But the victory at Orleans has rendered them glorious and honorable, be they what they may."

Republicans boasted of how they had defeated "the heroes of Wellington," "Wellington's *invincibles*," and "the conquerors of the conquerors of Europe." The myth of American victory continued to grow so that by 1816 *Niles' Register* could unabashedly claim that "we did virtually dictate the Treaty of Ghent."

As the years slipped by, most people forgot the causes of the war. They forgot the defeats on land and sea and lost sight of how close the nation had come to military and financial collapse. According to the emerging myth, the United States had won the war as well as the peace. The War of 1812 thus passed into history not as a futile and costly struggle in which the United States had barely escaped defeat and disunion but as a glorious triumph in which the nation had single-handedly defeated the conqueror of Napoleon and the Mistress of the Seas.

CHRONOLOGY

US	=	United States
USS	=	United States Ship
GB	=	Great Britain
HMS	=	His Majesty's Ship (British)
FR	=	France
RU	=	Russia
(n)	=	Number of guns on ship

1789–1801	Federalists in power
1789	
April 30	George Washington inaugurated as president
July 14	French Revolution begins
1789–91	US adopts Alexander Hamilton's financial program
1793 February 1	GB and FR go to war
1794 November 19	US and GB sign Jay Treaty
1797 March 4	John Adams inaugurated as president
1798–1801	US and FR in Quasi-War
1801–15+	Republicans in power
1801	
March 4	Thomas Jefferson inaugurated as president
October 1	GB and FR sign Treaty of Amiens
1801–2	US adopts retrenchment policy
1803 May 16	GB and FR resume war
1806	
April 18	US adopts partial nonimportation law
December 31	US and GB sign Monroe-Pinkney Treaty

1807

March	US rejects Monroe-Pinkney Treaty
June 22	*Chesapeake* affair
December 22	US adopts embargo

1807–9

	GB adopts Orders in Council

1809

March 1	US adopts nonintercourse law
March 4	James Madison inaugurated as president

1811

March 2	US adopts nonimportation law
May 16	*Little Belt* affair
November 4	War Congress convenes
November 7	Battle of Tippecanoe
November 12	US and GB settle *Chesapeake* affair
December–April	US adopts war preparations

1812

March 9	Madison exposes Henry plot
April 4	US adopts ninety-day embargo
April 14	US adopts ninety-day nonexportation law
May 19	USS *Hornet* returns from Europe
May 27	GB offers US share of license trade
June	FR invades RU
June 1	Madison sends war message to Congress
June 4	US House adopts war bill
June 16	GB announces plans to suspend Orders in Council
June 17	US Senate adopts war bill
June 18	Madison signs war bill (War of 1812 begins)
June 18–26	US sends out peace feelers
June 23	GB repeals Orders in Council
June–August	Baltimore riots
July 1	US doubles customs duties
July 6	US adopts first enemy trade law
July 16	British squadron captures USS *Nautilus* (14)
July 17	GB captures Mackinac
July–August	New England refuses to call out militia
August 9	Henry Dearborn signs armistice
August 13	USS *Essex* (46) captures HMS *Alert* (20)

August 15	Fort Dearborn massacre
August 16	GB captures Detroit
August 19	USS *Constitution* (54) defeats HMS *Guerrière* (49)
August 26	US repudiates Dearborn's armistice
October 9	US captures HMS *Detroit* (6) and HMS *Caledonia* (2)
October 13	Battle of Queenston
October 15	USS *United States* (56) defeats HMS *Macedonian* (49)
October 18	USS *Wasp* (18) defeats HMS *Frolic* (16)
October 18	HMS *Poictiers* (74) captures USS *Wasp* (18)
Fall	FR retreats from RU
Fall	Madison wins reelection
November	GB blockades South Carolina and Georgia
November 22	HMS *Southampton* (32) captures USS *Vixen* (14)
November 23	US retreats from eastern Canada
November 27	US attacks outlying positions at Fort Erie
December 26	GB proclaims blockade of Chesapeake and Delaware bays
December 29	USS *Constitution* (54) defeats HMS *Java* (49)

1813

January 22	Battle of Frenchtown
January 23	River Raisin massacre
February 9	Creeks attack US settlement on Duck River
February 24	USS *Hornet* (18) defeats HMS *Peacock* (18)
March 8	RU makes mediation offer
March 28	HMS *Phoebe* (46) and HMS *Cherub* (26) capture USS *Essex* (46)
April 15	US occupies part of West Florida
April 27	Battle of York
May 1–9	Siege of Fort Meigs
May 26	GB blockades additional middle and southern states
May 27	Battle of Fort George
May 29	Battle of Sackets Harbor
June 1	HMS *Shannon* (52) defeats USS *Chesapeake* (50)
June 5	Battle of Stoney Creek
June 22	Battle of Norfolk
June 24	Battle of Beaver Dams
June 26	GB attacks Hampton
July 24–August 2	US adopts internal taxes
July 27	Battle of Burnt Corn
August 2	US adopts law barring use of enemy licenses

August 2	Battle of Fort Stephenson
August 14	HMS *Pelican* (11) defeats USS *Argus* (10)
August 30	Battle of Fort Mims
September 5	USS *Enterprise* (16) defeats HMS *Boxer* (14)
September 10	Battle of Lake Erie
October 5	Battle of the Thames
October 16–19	Battle of Leipzig (in Europe)
October 26	Battle of Chateaugay
November 3	Battle of Tallushatchee
November 4	GB offers US direct peace negotiations
November 9	Battle of Talladega
November 11	Battle of Chrysler's Farm
November 16	GB extends blockade to all middle and southern states
December 10	US evacuates Fort George and burns Newark
December 17	US adopts embargo
December 18	GB captures Fort Niagara
December 18	GB destroys Lewiston and nearby towns

1814

January 22	Battle of Emuckfau
January 24	Battle of Enotachopco Creek
March 27–28	Battle of Horseshoe Bend
March 31	European allies enter Paris
April 11	Napoleon abdicates throne
April 14	US repeals embargo and nonimportation law
April 20	HMS *Orpheus* (36) captures USS *Frolic* (22)
April 25	GB extends blockade to New England
April 28	USS *Peacock* (22) defeats HMS *Epervier* (18)
June 22	HMS *Leander* (50) captures USS *Rattlesnake* (16)
June 28	USS *Wasp* (22) defeats HMS *Reindeer* (19)
July–September	GB occupies eastern Maine
July 3	US captures Fort Erie
July 5	Battle of Chippewa
July 12	HMS *Medway* (74) captures USS *Syren* (16)
July 25	Battle of Lundy's Lane
August	US public credit collapses
August	US banks suspend specie payments
August 8	Peace negotiations begin in Ghent
August 8–19	GB outlines initial peace terms
August 9	US and Creeks sign Treaty of Fort Jackson
August 14	GB occupies Pensacola

August 15	Battle of Fort Erie
August 24	Battle of Bladensburg
August 24–25	GB burns Washington
August 28	Nantucket declares neutrality
September 1	USS *Wasp* (22) defeats HMS *Avon* (18)
September 11	Battle of Plattsburgh
September 11	Battle of Lake Champlain
September 12	Battle of Mobile Bay
September 12	Battle of North Point
September 13–14	Battle of Baltimore
September 14	Francis Scott Key writes "The Star-Spangled Banner"
September 17	US sortie from Fort Erie
September 26	British squadron captures *General Armstrong* (9)
October 11	HMS *Endymion* (40) attacks *Prince-de-Neufchatel* (17)
October 21	GB offers peace on basis of *uti possidetis*
November 5	US evacuates Fort Erie
November 7	US occupies Pensacola
November 27	GB drops *uti possidetis*
December 14	Battle of Lake Borgne
December 15– January 5	Hartford Convention
December 15– February 27	US adopts additional internal taxes
December 23– January 1	Preliminary battles around New Orleans
December 24	US and GB sign Treaty of Ghent
December 28	US rejects conscription proposal

1815

January 8	Battle of New Orleans
January 15	British squadron defeats USS *President* (52)
February 4	US adopts second enemy trade law
February 11	Treaty of Ghent reaches US
February 16	US Senate approves Treaty of Ghent
February 16	Madison approves Treaty of Ghent
February 17	US rejects national bank proposal
February 17	US and GB exchange ratifications (War of 1812 ends)
February 20	USS *Constitution* (52) defeats HMS *Cyane* (34) and HMS *Levant* (20)
February 21	US executes 6 Tennessee militiamen
March 23	USS *Hornet* (20) defeats HMS *Penguin* (19)
April 6	Dartmoor massacre

Map 1. The Northern Theater

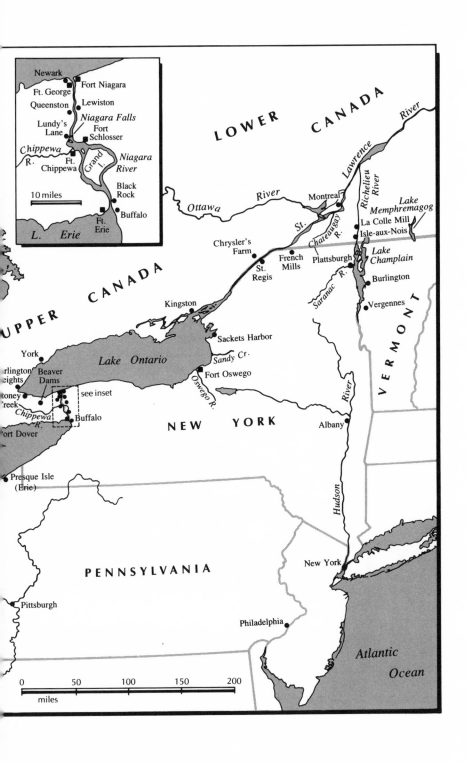

Inset:

Newark
Ft. George
Fort Niagara
Queenston
Lewiston
Niagara Falls
Lundy's Lane
Fort Schlosser
Chippewa R.
Ft. Chippewa
Grand I.
Niagara River
Black Rock
Buffalo
Ft. Erie
L. Erie

10 miles

Main map:

LOWER CANADA

River

Ottawa

River

St.

St. Lawrence River

Montreal

Richelieu River

Lake Memphremagog
La Colle Mill
Isle-aux-Nois

Chrysler's Farm

Chateaugay R.

Lake Champlain

St. Regis

French Mills

Plattsburgh

Saranac R.

Burlington

Vergennes

UPPER CANADA

Kingston

Lake Ontario

Sackets Harbor

Sandy Cr.

Fort Oswego

Oswego R.

River

V E R M O N T

York

Burlington Heights

Beaver Dams

Stoney Creek

Chippewa R.

Buffalo

see inset

Fort Dover

N E W   Y O R K

Albany

Presque Isle (Erie)

Hudson

P E N N S Y L V A N I A

Pittsburgh

Philadelphia

New York

Atlantic Ocean

0   50   100   150   200
miles

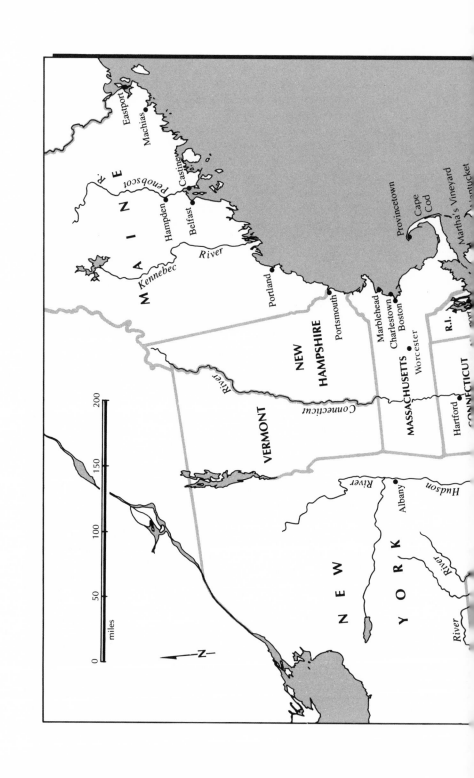

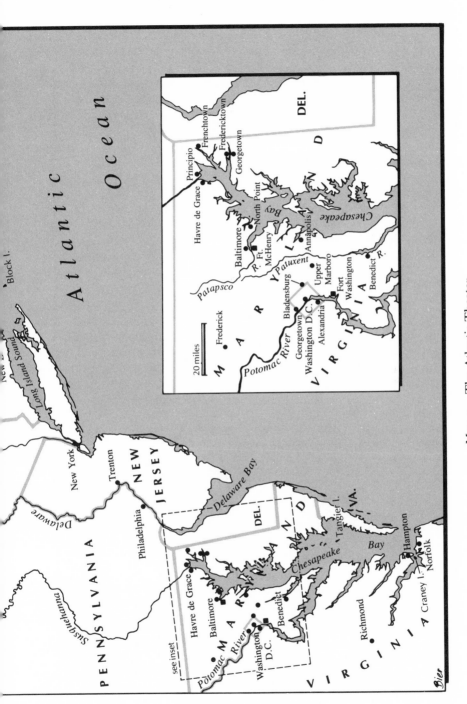

Map 2.   The Atlantic Theater

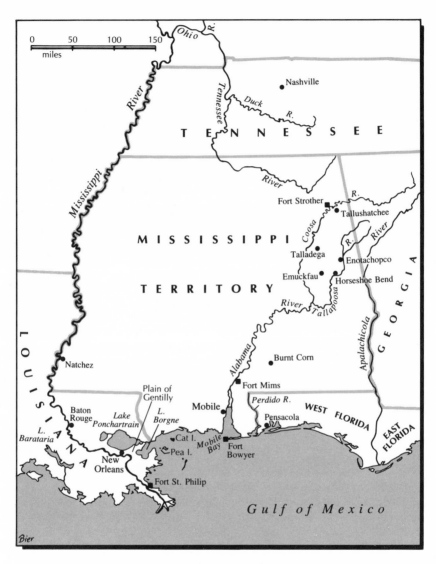

Map 3. The Southern Theater

SUGGESTIONS FOR FURTHER READING

The best starting point for any reading on the War of 1812 is a bibliography. The most useful are John C. Fredriksen, *Free Trade and Sailors' Rights: A Bibliography of the War of 1812* (1985); Dwight L. Smith, *The War of 1812: An Annotated Bibliography* (1985); and the list of sources at the end of John K. Mahon's *The War of 1812* (1972).

There are several good military histories of the war. The three best are John K. Mahon's *War of 1812* (1972), which is the most detailed; Reginald Horsman, *The War of 1812* (1969), which is the most accurate; and Harry L. Coles, *The War of 1812* (1965), which is the liveliest. Also valuable are Glenn Tucker's *Poltroons and Patriots: A Popular Account of the War of 1812*, 2 vols. (1954); and James R. Jacobs and Glenn Tucker, *The War of 1812: A Compact History* (1969). Allan S. Everest, *The War of 1812 in the Champlain Valley* (1981), is a good regional study.

The best accounts of the war at sea are still Theodore Roosevelt, *The Naval History of the War of 1812*, 2 vols., 3d. ed. (1900), which judiciously treats the battles; and Alfred T. Mahan, *Sea Power and Its Relations to the War of 1812*, 2 vols. (1905), which deals with the larger issues of naval strategy.

The best study of privateering is Edgar S. Maclay, *A History of American Privateers* (1899). Jerome R. Garitee, *The Republic's Private Navy: The American Privateering Business as Practiced by Baltimore during the War of 1812* (1977), is a good study of the in-port side of privateering.

For the domestic history of the war, Henry Adams, *A History of the United States during the Administrations of Jefferson and Madison*, 9 vols. (1889–91), has long been standard, though Adams sought to make almost everyone look bad except his ancestors, John Adams and John

Quincy Adams. The best antidote to Henry Adams is Irving Brant, *James Madison,* 6 vols. (1941–61), though this work goes too far in defending Madison.

For additional details on the domestic history, readers should consult my longer work, *The War of 1812: A Forgotten Conflict* (1989), which discusses the political, economic, and financial history of the war; and J. C. A. Stagg's *Mr. Madison's War: Politics, Diplomacy, and Warfare in the Early American Republic, 1783–1830* (1983), which traces the inner history of the Republican party and explores the impact of politics on the prosecution of the war.

INDEX

Donald R. Hickey received his Ph.D. in history from the University of Illinois at Urbana-Champaign in 1972. He has taught at the University of Illinois, the University of Colorado, the University of California at Santa Barbara, Texas Tech University, and the U.S. Army Command and General Staff College. He is currently a professor of history at Wayne State College in Nebraska. He is the author of *The War of 1812: A Forgotten Conflict* (1989), which is a longer version of the present work, and *Nebraska Moments: Glimpses of Nebraska's Past* (1992).